Founder, Fighter, Saxon Queen

In memory of my Uncle Simon
who loved medieval history and admired strong women

Founder, Fighter, Saxon Queen

Aethelflaed, Lady of the Mercians

Margaret C. Jones

PEN & SWORD
HISTORY

First published in Great Britain in 2018 by
PEN AND SWORD HISTORY
an imprint of
Pen and Sword Books Ltd
47 Church Street
Barnsley
South Yorkshire S70 2AS

ISBN 978 1 52673 396 2

Printed and bound in the UK
by T J International, Padstow, Cornwall, PL28 8RW

Typeset in Times New Roman by
Aura Technology and Software Services, India

Pen & Sword Books Ltd incorporates the imprints of Pen & Sword
Archaeology, Atlas, Aviation, Battleground, Discovery,
Family History, History, Maritime, Military, Naval, Politics, Railways,
Select, Social History, Transport, True Crime, Claymore Press,
Frontline Books, Leo Cooper, Praetorian Press, Remember When,
Seaforth Publishing and Wharncliffe.

For a complete list of Pen and Sword titles please contact
Pen and Sword Books Limited
47 Church Street, Barnsley, South Yorkshire, S70 2AS, England
E-mail: enquiries@pen-and-sword.co.uk
Website: www.pen-and-sword.co.uk

Contents

List of Illustrations

Preface

'She's buried in my back garden.'

This casual remark in a Gloucester lecture room caused heads to turn, and surprised laughter to ripple round the hall. That Aethelflaed, daughter of King Alfred the Great was claimed to have her last resting place behind a private house in a quiet Gloucester back street, might sound delusional, the grandiose brag of a fantasist. But the St Mary's Street resident had a case. His garden, like that of his next door neighbour Rebecca Trimnell, overlooks the ruins of St Oswald's, founded as a church in the tenth century. The founder was Aethelflaed. For seven years after her husband's death until her own in AD 918, this strong-minded woman ruled over the Anglo-Saxon kingdom of Mercia, a territory that stretched from Gloucester to Northumbria, and from Derby to the Welsh borders.

The first point to strike those who have written about Aethelflaed from the twelfth century to the present, is that she did what no Anglo-Saxon woman before her had done – she led her army in battle. But no Anglo-Saxon woman was expected to negotiate treaties either, or to be a town planner, or, in widowhood, to rule a kingdom in her own right – to collect taxes, hear appeals and administer the law. These aspects of the career of the Lady of the Mercians, as she was known to her subjects, are where Aethelflaed's real achievement lies. Many decisions that she took, in the previously unheard-of role of de facto queen of Mercia, changed the face of England.

To come back to Gloucester: Aethelflaed and her husband had arranged to be buried in a crypt at the eastern end of St Oswald's, in an area now covered by potting sheds and private lawns. An archaeological dig on this site in the mid-1970s uncovered the remains of thick stone walls. They appeared to mark the sides of a freestanding building, quite possibly the royal mausoleum. Treacherously sliding loose sand made it risky to excavate further, however, and the diggers gave up.

That we can't be certain exactly where Aethelflaed was buried hardly matters. Her name lives on. The Lady of the Mercians was a queen in all but name – and the Irish, who admired her, called her just that. Like her more famous father, she is great in her own right. She fought against Viking raiders, and built fortified towns to protect her people from attack. For the part she played in preparing her Midlands kingdom to become part of a unified England, she has been called England's 'founding mother'.

When her husband died in AD 911, Aethelflaed inherited the rule of a war-ravaged land. Under continuing attack from Danish and Norse Vikings, she drove back the raiders, and brought Danish-occupied parts of Mercia back under Mercian control. A skilled diplomat, she negotiated treaties with her neighbours – even with former enemies, when the time was right – to create a safer world for her people. In the conditions of peace made possible by her rule, industry and trade flourished. She founded shrines and churches. Most importantly for us, her inheritors, she fortified towns all across Mercia, and built new ones, protecting the inhabitants from attack and enabling these protected enclaves to prosper and grow.

Her building programme transformed the landscape. Many of the urban centres we know today – Chester, Stafford, Shrewsbury, Tamworth, Warwick – are Aethelflaed's gift to the Midlands. When you walk along the High Street in Warwick, or stroll around the four crowded and lively intersecting streets at the heart of Gloucester, you are following urban layouts decreed by the Lady of the Mercians.

There had been powerful Anglo-Saxon queens before Aethelflaed, exercising power as the wife of a king; and this was particularly true of Mercia. But Aethelflaed's choice to rule alone after her husband's death, instead of retiring quietly to a nunnery as royal widows were usually expected to do, was unique. Still more radical, was her attempt before her own death, to pass on the rule of Mercia to her daughter Aelfwynn. One woman would not again succeed another on a throne in England for 600 years – when Elizabeth I inherited the title of queen after the death of Mary Tudor.

Written out of the history books all through the nineteenth century, Aethelflaed is still honoured in the Midlands towns she founded. In recent years her story has been rediscovered by feminist historians, and by romantic novelists. No doubt the 1,100th anniversary of her death in 2018, will make many familiar with her name. Planning for the event is already under way in Tamworth, and in Gloucester, with proposals for the erection of a new statue to Aethelflaed,

In thinking about Aethelflaed's remarkable life and achievements for the writing of this book, I have had also to think about the world that made her. It is one full of paradox. The Anglo-Saxons in the kingdoms of Mercia, Wessex, East Anglia and Northumbria – the latter two subject to Danish rule when Aethelflaed was born – were a Christianised people. Yet they were still culturally close to their pre-Christian traditions and beliefs. This very sense of connectedness to the not-so-remote pagan past made them eager to distinguish themselves from their pagan enemies, the Danish and Norse peoples, whom the Anglo-Saxons often referred to in their writings as 'the heathen'. In their day-to-day religious practices, Aethelflaed's people were almost obsessively devout. And they subscribed, in theory at least, to Christian teachings of non-violence and turning the other cheek. Yet the brutal conditions of their war-torn world drove them to fight and kill – an activity sanctioned and celebrated in the heroic warrior traditions of their pre-Christian heritage.

Anglo-Saxon rulers were chosen by election, by a consensus of their nobles and high-ranking religious leaders. It was a democratic process that operated at the apex of society. However, their social world as a whole was profoundly unequal and hierarchical. Slavery was an accepted fact of life.

Not unlike the Victorians, they found no difficulty in combining piety and materialism. Though genuinely and intensely religious, their royal families saw no contradiction with their faith in appointing family members to head abbeys and convents, or in reaping financial profits from these institutions. Anglo-Saxon bishops owned large tracts of land, got into property disputes with other clergy, engaged in trade, and even minted their own coins.

Like the Victorians, too, Aethelflaed's people were great charitable givers, and great builders – of abbeys and churches, as well as of bridges and fortified towns. In both these respects, Aethelflaed was typical of her culture.

The church buildings she founded have not survived. Later generations erased that earlier architectural heritage, setting up new structures on the old Anglo-Saxon sites. Even if the building's architecture has changed beyond recognition, however, and the church is now dedicated to a different saint, in many cases the original ground of an 'Aethelflaed' church is still in religious use, with unbroken continuity through the centuries.

What we know about Aethelflaed's world in general, comes to us from the dedicated work of archaeologists – at forts, burial grounds, and in the foundations of houses; and from the often beautiful Anglo-Saxon artefacts – religious books, ornaments, weapons, jewellery, pottery and carved stone. Most informative, perhaps, are the writings that survive – sermons and prayers, poetry, legal documents, chronicles. These tell us so much, not only about how the Anglo-Saxons lived, in material terms, but how they felt and thought.

We know about Aethelflaed herself from the 'Mercian Register' of the *Anglo-Saxon Chronicles*, a handful of pages inserted into the *Chronicles'* main text; and from a few charters – records of grants of land, or other rights, in which her name appears. Bishop Asser's *Life* of Aethelflaed's father King Alfred gives us a little information about her family and the kind of education she probably received. Eleventh- and twelfth-century chronicles – the *Fragmentary Annals of Ireland*; William of Malmesbury's *Chronicle of the Kings of England*; Caradoc of Llancarvan's *History of Wales* – add legends about Aethelflaed that, even if we need to treat them with a pinch of scepticism, give a good sense of her intelligence, her courage, and the heroic reputation that grew around her, even in her lifetime.

Her legend remained popular in the Middle Ages; but over the centuries was eclipsed by the towering reputation of her more famous father. The citizens of Stafford and Tamworth remembered her again in 1913, when they celebrated her role in their founding a thousand years earlier. There were commemorative plays and pageants, and the erection of a statue to Aethelflaed in Tamworth. By then, however, the Lady of the Mercians had otherwise almost wholly vanished from recorded history. Hutchinson's popular *Story of the British Nation,* published in 1922, gave her a mention – but after that, for over thirty years the written record goes blank.

The first twentieth-century academic historian to take an interest in Aethelflaed, was F.T. Wainwright, whose article, 'Aethelflaed Lady of the Mercians', when it appeared in 1959 in a collection of scholarly essays, began a modest revival among academic historians. But it was still possible, even as late as the 1990s, to read a history of Anglo-Saxon England that dealt with King Alfred and his male descendants, but made no mention whatever of his heroic daughter. Then, in 1993, Don Stansbury published *The Lady Who Fought the Vikings,* the first full-length biography of Aethelflaed, and it became more common for historians of the Anglo-Saxon past to make at least passing mention of her. Ian Walker's chapter on Aethelflaed in *Mercia and the Making of England* (2000); Mary Dockray-Miller, with an essay in her feminist study, *Motherhood and Mothering in Anglo-Saxon England,* published the same year; Paul Hill, in his 2004 biography of Aethelflaed's nephew, *The Age of Athelstan,* all make this gesture.

Jane Wolfe, in 2001, produced a thirty-page booklet about Aethelflaed – *Royal Lady, War Lady.* Joanna Arman's briskly-paced *The Warrior Queen* (2017), is the first full-length biography of Aethelflaed since Stansbury. It pursues a number of intriguing lines of enquiry about Aethelflaed's and Alfred's family connections. Meanwhile, in his 2013 television documentary for the BBC, Michael Wood has probably done more to inform the general public about the Lady of the Mercians than a thousand printed pages.

The same might be said of *The Last Kingdom,* the recent dramatisation of Bernard Cornwell's novels about Anglo-Saxon

England televised by the BBC, except that viewers are likely to take away a somewhat misleading conception regarding the events of Aethelflaed's life. (She never was kidnapped by Vikings, for instance, as far as we know; or if she was, she kept very quiet about it.)

The Making of Aethelflaed considers the 'making' of the Lady of the Mercians from three perspectives: the world that made her – the one she grew up in, and that shaped her personality; the world she made, as a ruler in Mercia; and the making of her legend in the years from her death until the present day.

The world that made her

The first three chapters of this book, and the later chapter titled 'Alfred's Daughter', focus on the cultural and familial world that shaped Aethelflaed's personality and beliefs. They consider experiences in her early life, and in the years of her marriage, that empowered her to become ruler of a kingdom. The three months of violence and displacement in her childhood, after the Viking attack that made her family refugees, surely left their mark, as did her upbringing in a time of constant threat of invasion. Chapter One, 'A Wartime Childhood', tells the story of this time.

Then there were the influences on her, during her upbringing, of her feminine world. My second chapter, 'Aethelflaed and her Sisters', discusses the ideals of Wessex womanhood that Aethelflaed either internalised or reacted against, and the teachings of her church on appropriate 'womanly' behaviour. There were many cultural expectations she would have had to challenge, to establish herself in the role of Lady of the Mercians. She could, however, also have turned to the role models offered by powerful female relatives, particularly her Mercian ancestors, who might suggest to her, directly or indirectly, what a high-status Anglo-Saxon woman could achieve in the world.

Aethelflaed worked in a collaborative relationship with her Mercian husband, on projects that trained her to rule and gave her the confidence to carry on alone as Lady of the Mercians, after Aethelred died. The work the couple did together in Mercia, and Aethelflaed's gradual assumption of power, even during her husband's lifetime, form the main theme of the third chapter, 'Marriage'.

'Alfred's Daughter', Chapter Six, returns to the theme of 'the world that made her', to reflect on ways in which Aethelflaed gained from the positive influence of King Alfred, as a parent and as a role model. In this regard, Aethelflaed's experience parallels that of powerful women in more recent times who were inspired by charismatic politician fathers.

The world she made

Chapters Four, Five and Seven are concerned with Aethelflaed as herself a maker. In 'Remaking Mercia', 'Lady of the Church', and 'Aethelflaed's (Missing) Daughter', Aethelflaed's work for Mercia is described. We see her fighting, fortifying towns, and founding new ones; building churches, making treaties with neighbouring rulers, and seeking to guarantee her legacy by having her daughter inherit the throne of Mercia after her death.

'Remaking Mercia', details Aethelflaed's achievements at the height of her powers, not only as a warrior, but in the day-to-day administration of Mercia, and in her founding of new towns across her kingdom. It reflects on how the growing prosperity of these urban centres benefited later generations.

The chapter titled 'Lady of the Church' revisits Aethelflaed's cultural roots in Mercia, to understand her relationship with ninth- and tenth-century Anglo-Saxon Christianity. It describes her endowment of churches and shrines in Mercia – activities that were important to Aethelflaed for both political and personal reasons. 'Aethelflaed's (Missing) Daughter' tells the story of the unfortunate Aelfwynn, after she briefly succeeded her mother on the Mercian throne. It discusses Aethelflaed's probable aspirations for her daughter, the reasons why these went unrealised, and Aelfwynn's likely fate after she was abducted from Mercia.

The making of her legend

'Legacy and Legend', the final chapter, examines what the world has made of Aethelflaed in the centuries since her death. It reviews various representations of her down the years: in medieval portraits and written chronicles; in twentieth-century pageants; in sculpture and stained glass; in twenty-first century advertisements that use her name to sell products; in novels, and in the shifting conceptions of Aethelflaed on the part of twentieth-century historians. Often, it is the warrior queen who is most vividly remembered, although recent historians have offered more nuanced and complex views.

For those who enjoy visiting sites of historic interest, I have appended a set of notes on 'Where to Find Her' – a short guide to places around the Midlands that still bear traces of Aethelflaed's life and work, or that have memorial tributes to her, in one form or another.

I have taken care that the basic facts of this narrative – dates, places, sequence of events – are as scrupulously accurate as I could make them. I hope, therefore, that academic historians who happen to turn my pages will not be too dismissive of the occasional imagined short scenes I have interjected into the work, to evoke key moments of Aethelflaed's life – her childhood exile, for example; her marriage; her death at Tamworth. These vignettes are, if you will, my contribution to the Making of Aethelflaed in legend – employing words to invoke her memory, where others have made use of stained glass, paint or stone. If by doing so I have kindled the imagination of readers to picture an Aethelflaed of their own as they read (consistent with the known data of her life), and to understand just how remarkable this woman was – and is – then my aim in writing the book will have been achieved.

Acknowledgements

Like the Lady of the Mercians herself, this book would never have come of age without diverse influences going into its making, and the support and encouragement of many.

Chris Chatterton, formerly mayor of Gloucester (now director of the city's Soldiers of Gloucestershire Museum), is passionate about Gloucester's history, and well informed about Aethelflaed. Chris kindly took time out of his busy schedule to share his considerable knowledge about the city's undeservedly neglected past. Rebecca Trimnell generously allowed me to invade her family's Christmas lunchtime, to inspect her garden and the likely site of Aethelflaed's burial. The erudite historians of Wednesbury shared their infectious enthusiasm about their town's allegedly 'Aethelflaedan' *burh*. Frank Caldwell, of Sandwell Council's Museums, Arts and Heritage Department; Sandwell's serving Poet Laureate Brendan Hawthorne; and local historian–researcher Peter Knowles, all helped in pointing me towards the site of the ancient fortress, and in tracking down Steve Field's Aethelflaed sculpture on the Caryatid Gate, when I was at a loss to find it.

Others have helped in more ways than one to bring the Anglo-Saxon world alive for me. Museum staff have been especially helpful – not least the Gloucester City Museum, which houses the ornate stone grave covers from St Oswald's Priory; and Chippenham's museum, where volunteer staff told me tales of artefacts found locally, about Saxon–Viking battles in that area, and of ongoing efforts to locate King Alfred's palace by the River Avon. I am indebted to Samantha Craig, Collections Officer at Hereford Museum, who explained the probable layout of the town's outer wall, and sent me a photo of the reconstructed Saxon palisade.

I am most grateful to Angela Sidwell, the artist who designed the imposing sculpture of Aethelflaed at Runcorn. Angela kindly shared information about the sculpture project, telling how local schoolchildren had helped her with the work. Thanks also to the sculpture's current custodians, Peter Bentham and the other staff at Runcorn's Brindley theatre, who sent photos, to the staff at Leicester Guildhall, who have allowed me to photograph their elegant twentieth-century image of Aethelflaed by Benjamin Fletcher, and to Jordan Cousins, editor of the *Tamworth Herald*, for permission to reproduce the newspaper's historic photographs of the 1913 Tamworth 'millenary'.

I am particularly obliged to Gambargin, the Australian artist who generously gave permission to reproduce his dramatic image of Aethelflaed on the march, from the website, 'Women War Queens'. Also to St Andrew's church, Churchdown, and to Chester Cathedral for photographs of their beautiful Aethelflaeds in stained glass. For visuals of Aethelflaed in advertising, I am indebted to Gwen Sanchirico of the Sacre Brew beer company, and the American artist Jose Carmona, for kindly allowing me to reproduce Carmona's compelling image of the Lady of the Mercians in war gear. Also to educational company E2BN, who have permitted me to use Anna Fenn's haunting imagined portrait of Aethelflaed from their History's Heroes website – and, of course, to Anna Fenn herself.

Without Candia McCormack, the *Cotswold Life* editor who published my 'Aethelflaed, Lost Lady of Gloucester', back in 2015, I doubt if this book would ever have got started.

Acknowledgements would be incomplete without mention of Marion Glastonbury, my friend and former colleague at the University of the West of England, and of Bob Dumbleton her partner, who brought searching scrutiny to bear on many of my ideas, and refused to let me take anything for granted.

Another astute scholar–critic, Professor Essam Fattouh, gave me much encouragement with *The Making of Aethelflaed,* along with

ACKNOWLEDGEMENTS

constructive feedback on the completed manuscript. For a whole year, he uncomplainingly digested a running monologue on Aethelflaed with his breakfast, lunch and tea. Even of a loving husband like Essam, this is a lot to ask. So thank you, as always, for being there for me.

A Note on Names

People's names

For the names of members of Alfred's family, I have used popularly accepted modern spellings, rather than the way they were originally written. So Aethelflaed's nephew is named as Athelstan, not 'Aethelstan'. For less well-known figures, like St Beorhthelm, though, I have kept closer to the earlier spellings.

At different times, the name of the Lady of the Mercians has been rendered as 'Ethelflaeda', 'Ethelfleda', or 'Ethelfled'. These days, most writers seem comfortable with 'Aethelflaed', as she herself spelt it. It's pronounced, 'Athel-fled'.

Place names

I refer to places by their modern names; only sometimes adding an Anglo-Saxon name that Aethelflaed would have known a place by, for clarification or where I think readers might find this of interest.

A few other words

Thegns
A lord's followers are often referred to as thegns (which rhymes with 'lanes').

A NOTE ON NAMES

Witan

The ruler's council of advisers is a witan. (First syllable rhymes with 'bit'.)

Fyrd

An Anglo-Saxon army is a fyrd, pronounced as in 'feared'.

Burh

The frequently mentioned fortified towns, the burhs, that Alfred and his children built to defend against the Vikings are the ancestors of modern *boroughs*. Say the Old English and the modern word as a northern speaker would, and there's little difference between them.

CHAPTER ONE

A Wartime Childhood

'You have hurled us back before the enemy. Our foes plunder us at will.'[1]

Not long after the Christmas of AD 878, a young girl and her family find themselves refugees in a war zone, in flight from a ruthless invader.

For the household of King Alfred of Wessex, Christmas at Chippenham is usually a joyful time. Larder shelves at the king's hunting lodge sag under the weight of crocks of mead, half hidden behind a thicket of dangling joints of venison. At meals in the great hall the king's guests and noble retainers drink, sing, brag and roar with laughter, their blood warmed with the strong drink that flows freely. They nearly drown out the voice of a musician reciting heroic legends to the plunking of a harp. The king's wife Ealhswith sits surrounded by her ladies, all dressed, like her, in their finest silks and furs, sipping imported Gaulish wine. Freed from adult surveillance, children run out laughing into the yard to pelt one another with snowballs.

They have just celebrated Twelfth Night, the last night of the Christmas season. Everyone attended Mass for the feast of Epiphany, when the three Magi were said to have brought gifts to the newly born Christ Child in the manger at Bethlehem. For those enjoying the feasting and fun, the holiday can't go on long enough. For the cooks and other household servants, on the other hand, an end to the holiday means a lifting of their burden of extra chores. Anyone who works the land thinks already of the ploughing and sowing in the weeks ahead, once melting snow has softened the ground.

For the king's eldest child, nearly 9 years old, the end of Christmas signals a return to work on her embroidery, overseen by Ealhswith her mother, and to the poems and passages in books of religious devotion Aethelflaed is expected to learn by heart with her tutors. King Alfred has always regretted not receiving more formal education in his youth, and is keen his children should be better taught.

The musician is nearing the end of his recital. His audience, well fed and sleepy with drink, have settled down and are listening quietly, if drowsily, to the rhythmic chant of the tale – now brutally cut short by screams from outside the hall.

Abruptly sobered, the guests sit rigid, all straining to listen. They hear shouts out there in the yard, but not what is being shouted. Then the clash of weapons. Terrified small children run back inside to cling to their mothers. A kitchen boy dashes in, yelling something about a storeroom, a fire. The guests look at one another in alarm, trying to make sense of it all. Chippenham is a fortified place, shielded too by a bend in the river. The bridge over the Avon is guarded at all times – where are the guards?

One word makes itself clear through the general uproar, and is taken up by others. 'Vikings'.

The Vikings are in the yard – nearly at the door. Strong arms snatch up the small girl Aethelflaed, and rush her outside. She finds herself hoisted up on the back of someone's horse. With sharp instructions to hold on tight to his belt, the rider, one of her father's *thegns* gallops away with her at unnerving speed. He slows down only when at a safe distance from the fighting that seems to have broken out all around the palace. Fire is coming from a roof somewhere, lighting up the sky with a lurid glow. Here in the dark protection of the woods, horses jostle around her in the darkness, treading uneasily, their rumps bumping against the behind of the horse she sits on. Urgent muted voices surround her, full of doubts, questions – what to do now, where to go? Her father is here with them now, her mother too, and a nurse, cradling her little brother Edward wrapped up in a blanket, shushing him to keep him from crying.

It might have happened like that – a surprise attack during an evening's feasting; when the attackers knew the company would be relaxed and off-guard, their heads befuddled with heavy food and strong drink, their weapons stacked outside the hall, out of immediate reach, as both law and custom required. It has even been suggested that some enemy within the palace arranged to open the way for the Vikings.[2] Or did the attack come in the small hours, while everyone was asleep? All the historical record tells us, is that shortly after Twelfth Night a large force – a so-called 'raiding-army' – that had been encamped in Gloucester for the winter, made a sudden surprise assault on the royal residence at Chippenham. There are no eyewitness accounts. What we can be sure of, is that it generated terror.[3]

The Vikings were the bogeymen of their time. Whenever their swift longships sailed in from Scandinavia to harry the English coasts, or travelled up English rivers, they left a trail of destruction in their wake. Everyone knew what Vikings on the rampage could do. They plundered, raped, killed unarmed men and women, or carried them off as slaves. They set fire to farms and churches, stole or smashed holy icons, broke open royal tombs in hopes of finding treasure. 'Be quiet and go to sleep now, or the Vikings will get you', one imagines a Saxon mother telling a restless child.

The Viking raid of 793 on the Northumbrian community of Lindisfarne and the slaughter of unarmed monks there, was just the beginning.

That horrific attack was still talked about almost a century later. A Northumbrian chronicler, Simeon of Durham, recorded the grim events:

> *they reached the church of Lindisfarne, and there they miserably ravaged and pillaged; they trod the holy things under their polluted feet, dug up the altars. and plundered all the treasures of the church. Some of the brethren they slew; some they carried off with them in chains; the greater number they stripped naked, insulted, and cast out of doors, and some they drowned in the sea. [4]*

3

At the time of the raid, an English monk named Alcuin was living at the court of the emperor Charlemagne in Aachen; but the terrible news reached him even there. Alcuin expressed not only dismay, but disbelief, that the peace in his homeland could be shattered like this – and by people coming from overseas:

> *It is nearly 350 years that we and our fathers have inhabited this most lovely land, and never before has such terror appeared in Britain as this we have now suffered at the hands of the heathen. Nor was it thought possible that such an inroad from the sea could be made.* [5]

Alcuin found a kindred spirit in the ancient words of Jeremiah. The Hebrew prophet not only knew all about the terror of sudden foreign invasion, but was able to make sense of the catastrophe in terms of divine judgement: 'Is it not your desertion of the Lord your God that brings all this upon you?' Like Jeremiah, Alcuin interpreted the onslaught of merciless enemies as God's punishment. The Viking massacre could only be God's instrument of divine retribution upon a sinful people.[6] Alcuin was not alone in seeing the hand of God behind the Viking raids. All Anglo-Saxons tended to view the raids in apocalyptic terms, as the *Anglo-Saxon Chronicles* for 793 bear witness:

> *This year came dreadful fore-warnings over the land of the Northumbrians, terrifying the people most woefully ... immense sheets of light rushing through the air, and whirlwinds, and fiery dragons flying across the firmament. These tremendous tokens were soon followed by a great famine: and not long after, on the sixth day before the ides of January in the same year, the harrowing inroads of heathen men made lamentable havoc in the church of God in Holy-island, by rapine and slaughter.* [7]

An Irish chronicler, writing two centuries later, drew similar conclusions. The churches in Ireland had, he claimed, been saved from Viking raiders who were burning and looting them and terrorising whole communities, by the fasting and prayers of a godly man named Céle Dabaill. The raids had been visited on the unfortunate people, the annalist believed, 'on account of the Lord's anger against them'. [8]

All over Europe, in those days of terror, the inhabitants of peaceful communities prayed much the same prayer: 'Deliver us, God, from the savage race of Northmen which lays waste our realms.' [9]

In 869, nine years before the assault on Alfred and his people in Chippenham, the pious king Edmund of East Anglia had been captured by invading Vikings, under the leadership of one Ivar, 'the Boneless'. According to the legends told about him many years later, Edmund knew he was militarily unprepared and outnumbered. He chose martyrdom at the hands of the Danes, rather than accept their demands for submission to them as overlords. His thegns, his personal entourage of loyal fighting men, had been killed with their families while they slept. He had no wish to live on as a puppet ruler of the Vikings. He would die with his people, and keep his Christian faith:

> This I desire ... that I should not be left alone after my dear thegns, who have been suddenly slain in their beds by these seamen, with their children and their wives. It has never been my custom to take to flight, but I would rather die, if I must, for my own land; and almighty God knows that I will never turn aside from His worship, nor from His true love, whether I die or live. [10]

The Vikings who surged into Chippenham were, like those who had murdered King Edmund nine years earlier, Danish. 'Viking' was simply a nickname given them by those on the receiving end of their violence, the raiders being famous for the 'wics' or temporary camps they set up, as they roved in search of new plunder. To 'go viking' was an activity, not an ethnic group. [11] Skilful seamen, Danes and Norsemen out viking crossed the North Sea in their shallow-draft longships, capable of carrying forty to fifty men at a time. They travelled up the great waterways of England – Thames, Humber, Severn – and entered the heartlands. They had the advantage over their Anglo-Saxon victims, of being unrestrained by any fear of Saxon reprisals against their families and farms, safely left behind in Scandinavia. No doubt they behaved no worse than many other armies invading a foreign land distant from home – including, it may be, the Anglo-Saxons when they had arrived in England and met with local resistance, some four centuries before the Vikings; or in more recent years, when Saxon armies were subduing uncooperative Celts on the Welsh borders. But this can have been small consolation to unfortunate people who found themselves trapped in the Vikings' path.

More invaders kept arriving. In AD 850 they brought 350 ships to moorings at the Isle of Thanet in Kent. They raided Canterbury, then London. Most disturbingly, they did not go back home, as in previous years, once the pillaging was done. This was to be the first of many years in which Vikings settled down in England for the winter. They were making plans for the long term.[12]

In 851, Alfred's father Aethelwulf, aided by his son Aethelbald, routed a Viking force, after it crossed into Surrey – but the respite was only temporary. This particular 'raiding-army' might have suffered a reverse; but others were on their way.

Viking attacks on English territory were moving inland with Viking forces growing in size. It was no longer a matter merely of pirate raids, where the raiders stayed just long enough to plunder and pillage, before sailing home with the spoils. What communities all across England now faced was what the *Anglo-Saxon Chronicle* termed the 'micel here', the 'great raiding-army'. It was not so much an army of raiders, in fact, but an invasion force, or rather successive waves of invaders, bent on conquest of territory. After torturing and killing King Edmund, the Vikings seized the whole kingdom of East Anglia. By 878 and the attack on Chippenham, the kingdoms of Mercia and Northumbria had fallen too. A Danish base established at

York quickly became a centre of Viking power in the northeast. Now, it seemed, it was the turn of Alfred, and of Wessex.

The Saxon defenders were out-manoeuvred by the Viking invaders at every turn. From a military point of view, the latter had several advantages over those they invaded. They operated in semi-autonomous war bands, each under the leadership of its own chief, or 'jarl'. They could travel fast across great swathes of country, seizing horses as they went. Wherever they went they set up bases, fortified garrisons and storehouses, seizing from terrified local people whatever they needed by way of supplies.

The Vikings were organised for war – the Anglo-Saxons in Wessex in the late ninth century, anything but. True, each great Saxon lord had his band of well-trained armed thegns, and the peasantry could be conscripted to fight at short notice. But these conscripts probably saw little point in getting too far from home, or in defending other men's crops and families, even with the promise of profit from looting slaughtered Vikings. When their term of service ended, provisions ran out, or the crops needed harvesting, they were apt to melt away.

Like their neighbours in East Anglia and Mercia, the West Saxons, overwhelmed by the ferocity and suddenness of acts of aggression for which they were wholly unprepared saw no choice but to buy off the Vikings by 'making peace' – paying their enemies to leave their territory; sometimes even supplying them with horses to go and raid someone else's land. This response to a ruthless and determined enemy was counterproductive, however. At best, it might buy the victims a little breathing space between raids. Finding 'making peace' an easier way of getting plunder than fighting for it, the raiders were all too likely to come back later for more.

Already, by the mid-800s, the kings of Wessex and neighbouring Mercia, long in rivalry, had begun to sink their differences to face the common threat. In 853 King Aethelfwulf of Wessex married off his daughter Aethelswith to the Mercian king, Burgred, to cement a military alliance between the two kingdoms. After Aethelwulf died in 858, it would be left to Aethelwulf's sons – Aethelbald, then his brothers Aethelberht, Aethelred and finally the youngest, Aethelflaed's father Alfred, to carry on the fight.

In 865 the largest army yet, a true 'micel here', arrived in southern England. The following year, having been bought off by the king in East Anglia, they went north and took York.

In 868, after an appeal for help from King Burgred, a 19-year-old Alfred rode with his older brother, King Aethelred of Wessex, to do battle against the Vikings in Mercia. A joint Wessex-Mercian force unsuccessfully besieged the Viking-held fortress at Nottingham. Then Alfred's brother Aethelred, who had succeeded to the throne of Wessex, was defeated by combined Danish forces at Reading. Aethelred died in 871, and Alfred (now married, and the father of a girl-child named Aethelflaed), succeeded him as king of Wessex. Alfred's victory over a Viking army at Ashdown in Berkshire shortly after his accession to the throne was followed by a crushing defeat at Wilton. It was a year of such defeats, King Alfred's friend and biographer Bishop Asser would say of it later. The warriors of Wessex were, he wrote, in the course of eight major battles, 'virtually annihilated to a man'.[13] Even allowing for a degree of exaggeration on Asser's part, it's clear that Alfred had a grim struggle on his hands. His little daughter grew up knowing her father might be called out to fight at any time, and that he might not come back.

Aetheflaed would have been about 5 when, in 874, her aunt Aethelswith's husband king Burgred of Mercia, was overthrown in a Danish Viking invasion. Burgred went into exile, and his wife with him. The Danes appointed a puppet king in Burgred's place.

In the winter of 876, when Aethelflaed was 7 or 8 and her father had been king for five years, the Vikings brought a massive invasion force into Wessex. They captured Wareham in Dorset, spreading out from there to plunder all across Dorset and Devon. Like other Saxon rulers before him, Alfred saw no alternative to 'making peace', by paying the invaders to go away. It was a 'peace' that lasted a few months only. When the Vikings seized control of Exeter, the king rode down to besiege them at the fortress they had established in the town.

Here luck, or providence, intervened. A sudden violent storm off Swanage in Dorset destroyed 120 of the Viking army's ships that had been moored there. So devastating was the loss for the invaders that Alfred was able to persuade them to leave Wessex, and retreat into Mercia. They set up camp for the winter in Gloucester, outside Wessex territory, but still uncomfortably close to the Wessex border. When they returned to the attack just weeks later, Chippenham was only thirty miles away.

How the raiders got there from their winter base in Mercia, is unknown. The seemingly most direct route, in a straight line from Gloucester, would be overland, a distance of roughly twenty-eight miles. That, however, would require travelling over the steep and thickly wooded Cotswolds – not impossible, but slow and heavy going in ice and snow. Or they might have sailed down the Severn from Gloucester, and up into the Avon. That would have taken them at least as far as Bath, before they came to frozen marshland that would have made it impossible to sail further. From Bath it was a fifteen-mile march north-eastwards to reach Chippenham. However they got there, they attacked in dead of winter, a time when most military activity normally came to a halt. They would have taken the Saxons completely by surprise.

Chippenham was a favourite royal residence with Alfred, who enjoyed hunting in the area. The Vikings may well have known he would be there over Christmas, and were looking for him and his family. The king had gained a reputation as a brave, stubborn adversary, who kept on fighting despite constant military defeats. To have killed or captured this Wessex king who held out against them when all other Anglo-Saxon kingdoms had fallen to Viking control, would have triumphantly completed the Danish conquest of England.

How did Aethelflaed's father react when the Vikings descended on his home? Did he draw his sword and try to kill a few of the attackers, before beating a retreat? Or did loyal retainers take that stand, giving their lives to enable the king to be surrounded by a protective body of men and hustled away to safety? The chronicles don't tell us. We only know he got away.

Alfred had had to make a choice. If he had stayed on at Chippenham to fight and been killed in battle there, he would have been the subject of epic poems and legends for centuries to come. If captured alive by the Vikings, he would have suffered a fate similar to that of the unfortunate King Edmund of the East Anglians, savagely flogged and shot to death with arrows, and been hailed as a saint.

The Wessex king was determined, however, to be neither a dead hero nor a martyr. He made a more pragmatic choice. By now, he knew, the Viking forces would have cut off all escape from Chippenham to the west and north. But the way to the south was still open, and Alfred took it.

And took his family with him?

Famously, he sought refuge on the island of Athelney, in the Somerset marshes – with a handful of trusted companions, according to the *Anglo-Saxon Chronicles* – a 'small troop' who 'went with difficulty through woods and into swamp-fastnesses'. Bishop Asser tells us a little more in his *Life* of the king: 'King Alfred, with a few men, made a fortress at a place called Athelney, and from it, with the thegns of Somerset, he struck out relentlessly and tirelessly against the Vikings.'[14] Were these 'few men' just that – all male companions, a chosen band of trusted warriors? Or did the king's immediate family join him in his marshland exile?

Where else could Aethelflaed, her mother, and other female relatives have gone for shelter? A monastery would hardly have been a safe refuge, given that the Vikings deliberately targeted such places. It was easy enough for them to set fire to wooden buildings, and to butcher everyone inside. Aethelflaed and her family would have felt about as safe in a monastery as modern refugees in a bomb store.

In a version of the apocryphal story of Alfred's vision of St Cuthbert, composed by William of Malmesbury in the twelfth century, Alfred is described as being accompanied to Athelney by his mother. In the legend, the saint not only assures Alfred that his kingdom will be restored to him, but comforts 'his mother also, who was lying near him ... with the same joyful intelligence'. Though fanciful, the narrative does suggest that Alfred's being accompanied by his family in his refuge, was not unthinkable.[15]

Images of Alfred's exile from Victorian times portray a lonely figure sitting hermit-like before his campfire in the solitude of the marshes. From his primitive wattle-and-daub hut, he ventures out from time to time – to infiltrate the Danish camp disguised as a minstrel; or, in a fit of absent-mindedness, to burn a peasant woman's cakes. The facts, as unearthed by recent excavations in Somerset, are rather different.

The small island in the Somerset marshes, about an acre and a half in size, was a fortified place in the Iron Age, hundreds of years before the Anglo-Saxons arrived in Britain. In Saxon times it became known as 'The Isle of Aethelings', or Princes' Island, after it served as the retreat of Aethelwine (later St Aethelwine), a seventh-century prince-turned hermit, said to be King Alfred's ancestor. Athelney, then, was a secure refuge, even in Alfred's time.

Bishop Asser's description of the place in his *Life* of Alfred was long thought to be a fantastic exaggeration. He wrote that the place was surrounded by '… swampy impassable and extensive marshland and ground water on every side'. The place 'cannot be reached in any way,' Asser said, 'except by punts or by a causeway'.[16]

Asser didn't meet King Alfred until seven years after the events he described, though there would surely have been plenty of people in Wessex ready to tell him about the retreat to Athelney, including Alfred himself. Excavations there in 2003 largely support Asser's description. The site was found to have been surrounded by a ditch, deepest at its most vulnerable points, shallower where the marshes would have made access more difficult, and probably supplemented by a wooden palisade. At the end of the causeway, that offered the only dry approach to the fort, would have been a gatehouse, behind a semi-circular external fence. Otherwise, the fort in winter could, as Asser says, have been approached only by boat. The impenetrable jungle of reed beds surrounding Athelney, and the treacherous marshy ground underfoot, would have made the place difficult to find, or to access, even for anyone who knew the island was there. Alfred's forces would have supplemented the existing defences in this basically secure retreat by erecting new palisades and putting up primitive shelters for the king, his followers and family.

Archaeological evidence from the 2003 excavations suggests the existence at Athelney of a metalworking forge, capable of producing sophisticated steel weapons. Here, Alfred would build an arsenal, preparing for a major fight-back against the Vikings in that spring of 878.

It seems likely he had kept Athelney in mind all along. The retreat to the Isle of Aethelings was no random panic flight, but action on a contingency plan to be carried out in case of emergency. That emergency had now arrived.

It was a fifty-mile journey from Chippenham down to Athelney. Alfred's party would have taken a wide detour round Bath in case the Danes were there. Wells and Glastonbury lay along their route south, although possibly difficult to access, other than by boat, in the winter floods. If anyone had been able to get there, however, they could have picked up a few supplies.

The alternative route would have been a long circular ride on higher ground, skirting around the lower slopes of the Mendips. In either case, it would have been a grim journey: the horses plunging through snowdrifts, slipping on slush and ice; their riders with set, sombre faces.

Some had left loved ones behind, dead in the palace yard, or simply gone missing. As yet, many of the survivors were too shocked and dazed by the sudden change in their lives even to count their losses. A lot of silent prayers were said. Aethelflaed, perhaps bundled up in a cloak someone had found for her, still clinging to the horseman's belt, was fighting not to drift off into frozen sleep. Other children and women rode close by, guarded by men with swords in case of sudden attack.

At Athelney, food was in short supply. The refugees lived on what they could forage, hunting and fishing in the woods and marshes, raiding Viking encampments, or taking what they needed from fellow-Saxons who had surrendered to the Vikings.

Alfred did not sit quietly inside his camp, sharpening his weapons and waiting for the spring. He used the fort as a base from which to move out on raids against the Vikings. If Aethelflaed and her family were with Alfred there, she daily heard atrocity stories about the Vikings' crimes; heard tales of raids and ambush – heard and saw groaning injured men carried back into the stronghold to die. In common with everyone else at Athelney, she could have no idea how, or when, or even if, this nightmare of embattled exile would end.

For long weeks after the king and his people took refuge in the fort, it looked as if the Vikings would seize permanent control of Wessex, as they had of neighbouring lands. With the king a refugee in hiding, the Danes soon occupied a great part of the kingdom, 'and very nearly all the residents of that region submitted to their authority'.

Alfred had left his subjects to the mercy of the invaders. He had little choice. Like his people, he found himself – in his own case rather literally – with his back to the wall. To the inhabitants of Wessex, though, it must have seemed their king had abandoned them.

Yet even at that moment of apparent total defeat, no one could have accused the king of cowardice – a man who had been in battle after battle against the Danes since his late teens. And still he was holding out. The Vikings, say the *Anglo-Saxon Chronicles*, 'over-rode and occupied the land of Wessex, and drove many of the people across the sea, and the greatest part of the others they over-rode – except Alfred the king'.[17] Like all his subjects, his daughter Aethelflaed would have to trust him.

Picture the child Aethelflaed in 878, at Athelney. Swaddled in her thick cloak, her long braided blonde hair wound about her neck as a makeshift scarf, she shivers in the early morning wind – thinks longingly of her comfortable bed left behind in Chippenham. Gazing out to where the mist hangs low over the reed beds, she watches the small birds perched on the reed stems fluffing out their feathers for warmth. As she stands there, her young heart pounds with dread. She wonders what will happen to them all.

Or is she unafraid? Does she even feel a certain excitement, at this sudden rupture in a humdrum life – wish she could go out with the men on their raids against the Vikings? This is Alfred's daughter, after all, brave child of a courageous father.

The Chippenham attack and the flight to Athelney have surely been formative moments for Aethelflaed, when the outside world burst with violence into the protected safety of her childhood. A hunted exile, she copes daily with hunger, cold, and uncertainty about her own and her family's future – with the question, indeed, of whether they have a future at all.

A childhood experience like hers – being driven from her home, living under constant threat of a cruel death – could have produced an anxious adult with a permanent sense of insecurity. Or it could bring forth an adult with a sense of mission – one who, having been driven from home and witnessed the killing of innocents, grows determined to put a stop to it. The latter seems to have happened to Aethelflaed.

She and her family never suffered the worst cruelties of the Viking invasions. Unlike many unfortunate peasant women, she was not subjected to torture, rape, or enslavement. None of her close relatives were killed, as far as we know, on or off the battlefield. If supplies ran short at Athelney, its inhabitants never experienced the horrors of a prolonged siege. Only the insecurity of never knowing what each day would bring; and that would have been hard enough.

The frosts began to melt. The blackthorn broke into flower, then leaf. The first leaves appeared on the hawthorns. The long fasting season of Lent – no doubt rendered especially poignant that year, when the fugitives on Athelney could well identify with the privations of Christ, hungry in the wilderness – had at last come to its end, with the celebration of Easter. In the pleasant sunshine, with all the trees in full leaf, the king decided the time had come to move out from hiding. Young though she was, Aethelflaed would have known when her father rode away from Athelney that day that he had gone to do battle with the Danes, and, with all the women left behind, would have prayed for him.

Alfred called his supporters to rally to him near Selwood in Wiltshire: 'In the seventh week after Easter he rode to Egbert's Stone ... and there came to join him all Somerset and Wiltshire and that part of Hampshire which was on this side of the sea, and they were glad of him.'[18] After a night's encampment, the combined forces marched to meet the Danish leader Guthrum at Edington in Wiltshire, where Guthrum was using the old hill fort of Bratton Castle as a temporary stronghold. [19]

It was a bitter fight, with many deaths on both sides. The king, 'fighting fiercely with a compact shield-wall against the entire Viking army... persevered resolutely for a long time'. Finally, though, Guthrum's forces broke and ran. Alfred and his army pursued them with his army, cutting down the fugitives from behind, the whole fifteen miles back to Chippenham. There he laid siege to the Vikings' fortress. After two weeks, they surrendered. Asser tells the rest of the story: 'The Vikings, thoroughly terrified by hunger, cold and fear, and in the end by despair, sought peace ... the king should take as many chosen hostages as he wanted from them and give none to them.'[20]

Never before, Asser remarks, 'had they made peace with anyone on such terms'. 'Moved to compassion', Alfred accepted the Viking surrender, on condition that Guthrum agreed to be baptised as a Christian; the king would act as the Danish leader's sponsor, 'receiving him as his adopted son'.[21] The treaty that followed the baptismal ceremony divided English lands into those under Saxon control, and the 'Danelaw' – giving de facto recognition of Danish control over East Anglia and the northeast.

If Aethelflaed's father thought that was the end of his troubles with Vikings, however, he was mistaken. Fighting with Danish invaders would continue, on and off, for years. In 892, a new land-hungry invasion force of Vikings sailed from mainland Europe, and up into the mouth of the Thames.

Aethelflaed was in her late teens by then, married, and living in Mercia. The by-now ageing Alfred took the field against the enemy for one last time, leading his army against the invaders in Kent. It was left to Aethelflaed's brother Edward, and to her husband, Aethelred of the Mercians, to carry on the fight.

Soon enough, it would be Aethelflaed's turn.

CHAPTER TWO

Aethelflaed and Her Sisters

'Embroidery is fitting for a woman. A woman who gads about attracts spiteful gossip ... often her beauty wanes.' [22]

Aethelflaed's earliest years were spent in a world of women. From the moment she was lifted free of Ealhswith's body, washed and wrapped in clean linen bands and given to her mother to hold, she was surrounded by female attendants. She was Ealhswith's first child, and the young mother would have turned to servants and family members for all the help and advice she could get. While the wet nurse fed baby Aethelflaed with milk from her own breast, other women came to talk to her, play with her, admire her – ladies in waiting, aunts, female cousins. Later they would carry her out to look at the garden, put her down on the floor, help her to crawl, to walk. Ealhswith was a constant hovering presence. Sometimes her father came to talk to and play with the child; but her day-to-day needs were met by slaves and servants.

A secure personality is formed in a child's early development by a sense of safety and love, a 'base' from which to explore the world, in the first years.[23] If Aethelflaed coped well with the trauma of the Viking raid at Chippenham and the subsequent months of exile, no doubt that owed much to security and warmth in her rearing as an infant.

In cultural settings where the early care of children is handed over from the biological mother to other people, these surrogate

16

carers can have a powerful influence. Any such early experiences of Aethelflaed's are, of course, lost to us. We can be fairly sure, though, that the world of her infancy was shaped by a close-knit community of women. Her wet nurse and other female carers may well have been more significant maternal figures for her, than Ealhswith.

As she grew older, Aethelflaed would see more of her mother, who would take an interest in teaching her to read. West Saxon and Mercian women of high status played a key part in instructing both their young sons and their daughters in literacy and other accomplishments. Bishop Asser's famous story of Aethelflaed's maternal grandmother encouraging her son Alfred to memorise a book of poems – whether in fact it ever happened as Asser tells it, or is merely the stuff of family folklore – illustrates the centrality of women to their children's education.[24] If, as Asser says, Alfred's own younger children had tutors to encourage their love of reading, they also had a well-educated mother. A confident woman like Ealhswith, descended from Mercian rulers, who at the end of her life would found an abbey in Winchester, would not only give her daughter a formal education; she would encourage in her eldest child the conviction that Aethelflaed might one day play some significant role in the world.[25]

Ealhswith was very pious, a trait she shared with her husband. Bishop Asser praises Alfred's 'excellent wife', as he calls her, for remaining single, 'a chaste widow', after her husband's death.[26] Ealhswith probably taught her daughter to say her prayers. In the company of her younger siblings, Aethelflaed would have gone to Mass; learned passages from the Gospels, and stories about the lives of the saints. (No doubt, as her younger brother Edward became old enough to play with, she enjoyed showing off to him her vast learning.)

Ealhswith's father was a high-ranking Mercian nobleman, Aethelred Mucil, an ealdorman of the Gaini people, in a sub-kingdom of Mercia. Eadburh, her mother, was a member of the Mercian royal family. Although she could have had no inkling of it in her childhood, these maternal connections would prove important to Aethelflaed in later life. When she left Wessex as the wife of Ealdorman Aethelred, they would make of her a Mercian among

Mercians, able to be accepted not as a foreigner, but as one of the people she would come to rule.

All that, however, was far in the future. As a young unmarried girl, Aethelflaed had other preoccupations. As she grew towards maturity there were social visits to make, clothes to choose, new babies to admire. There were embroidery sessions with her sisters and the ladies of the court. All women, from the humblest to the highest in status, were taught to sew. Aristocratic women with time on their hands and no need to make clothes for use, would still learn to embroider beautifully. (Sadly, most of this work has not survived the ravages of time.)[27]

There were outdoor activities too – riding, and hawking. There were alms to be donated to the church and to the poor, christenings and weddings to attend – and funerals, all too many of them, following the untimely deaths of children in an age when infant mortality was high.

Other women's lives would have been dissected in detail. Some women were to be admired and imitated, others dismissed with scorn. What traits a woman might aspire to, what behaviour to avoid, was something Aethelflaed would absorb almost unconsciously from her surroundings.

Apart from Ealhswith, two other prominent female family members are likely to have been important role models for Aethelflaed as she grew – Osburh her paternal grandmother, and her father's sister, Aethelswith.

Alfred's mother Osburh was said to be 'a most religious woman, noble in character and noble by birth'. Her father Oslac had been Aethelwulf's 'cup bearer' – his butler or steward – an official and highly honourable position. Even so, Osburh's status in relationship to Alfred's father Aethelwulf seems to have been quite tenuous. She may have been 'set aside' in 856 –'dismissed' from Aethelwulf's 'sexual service', in favour of the king's new bride Judith, adolescent daughter of the Frankish king Charles.[28] All the same, she would have been still in her mid- to late thirties when Aethelflaed was born, and could have played a part in Aethelflaed's life, as she had in that of her young son Alfred. Whether or not, as William of Malmesbury has it,

Osburh went with Alfred into exile at Athelney, that she was around in Alfred's court during Aethelflaed's childhood is quite likely. Even if Aethelflaed never met her grandmother in person, she would certainly have heard about her from her father.[29]

Beyond the spare description given by Asser in his *Life* of Alfred, however, almost nothing is known about Osburh personally. Like other ninth-century Wessex royal woman, as far as her public presence goes, she remains 'cloaked in silence'. The most important fact about her in relation to Aethelflaed is that, as the story of Alfred and the poetry book suggests, Osburh, like her daughter-in-law Ealhswith, was an educated woman who liked to teach.[30]

Another older female relative with Mercian connections, was Aethelflaed's aunt Aethelswith, who would have known Aethelflaed's mother well. Aethelswith had been married off to King Burgred of Mercia to seal a political and military alliance between Mercia and Wessex. She shared power with Burgred in Mercia for twenty-one years, until invading Vikings drove her husband from his throne and his kingdom in 874. Aethelswith fled with Burgred. Quite likely she went with him to Rome, where her husband died shortly after being driven into exile. Whether she remained there after his death is questionable. Though Aethelswith herself died in Italy – fourteen years later, at Pavia – it is possible that she had before then been living at the court of her brother Alfred in Wessex. (She may have been travelling back towards Rome on pilgrimage, when her life ended at Pavia.) If she had returned to Alfred's court, Aethelflaed certainly would have known her, and been influenced by her.

As a queen in Mercia before the Viking takeover, Aethelswith had been a powerful figure in her own right. She is recorded as having witnessed six surviving charters – legal decrees, contracts for grants of land, and other financial transactions. Three surviving documents show her actually issuing charters – two jointly with her husband, and one in her own right. On each of these documents she is named as 'Aethelswith Regina' – Queen Aethelswith.

One of the Anglo-Saxon treasures of the British Museum is an ornately worked ring found at Aberford in Yorkshire, bearing

Aethelswith's name. This rare and unusual object, too large to be worn on even a very large finger, too small to be any kind of bracelet, is thought to be a ceremonial gift of some kind. If so, it denotes Aethelswith as, in the legendary tradition of powerful Anglo-Saxon rulers, a 'ring-giver', whose royal generosity conferred honour on those who received it. Aethelswith could have offered Aethelflaed insight into a world more liberated than that of Wessex, where royal women might exercise a good deal of political power.[31]

Aethelflaed had four siblings who survived into adulthood: her younger brothers, Edward and Aethelweard, and her two younger sisters, Aethelgifu and Aelfthryth. The fates of these two women dramatically highlight and contrast with the path followed by their older sister, who so decisively challenged the conventional expectations of West Saxon womanhood. Aethelflaed's sisters lived out the usual destinies of most high-status women in ninth-century England, generally decided for them by their families at an early age. Aelfthryth would marry into the Flemish aristocracy, becoming the wife of Baldwin II, Count of Flanders. Aethelgifu was made abbess of a newly founded nunnery at Shaftesbury in Dorset. (She died in her early twenties, outlived by both her parents; which must have been a source of great grief to them.)

Ealhswith had given birth to other children who died in infancy. Childbearing, for both mother and baby, was as dangerous as combat on the battlefield – possibly more so. Hearing of the death of a newborn, or of a mother while giving birth, must have been a common event for Aethelflaed. One has to wonder whether the atmosphere of pain and loss affected her own attitudes to childbearing in adulthood, and contributed to her reluctance to bear children?

Along with the influences of female relatives, Aethelflaed was also immersed in the traditions of her culture – the folklore and legends of her community, the poems she read and memorised, tales of female saints, homilies and other formal teachings of the church. Many of these carried explicit or implicit messages about ideal feminine behaviour, or stern warnings about what a virtuous woman should avoid. Which is not to say that the message would necessarily be interpreted as the messenger intended.

In Wessex, as suggested previously, even royal women were firmly subjected to male authority and accorded a lower status than their male kin. Asser gives us a glimpse of this, when he writes of the subordinate status of a king's wife in Wessex: 'For the West Saxons did not allow the queen to sit beside the king, nor indeed did they allow her to be called "queen", but rather "king's wife".' Asser, a Welshman familiar with Celtic societies in which royal and aristocratic women were powerful, had no time for the patriarchal conservatism of the rulers of Wessex, 'This perverse and detestable custom, contrary to the practice of all Germanic peoples', he calls the West Saxon custom regarding the wife of a king.[32]

An exception to the rule was made in Wessex, when Aethelflaed's grandfather Aethelwulf married the 14-year-old Judith, daughter of Charles the Bald, king of the Franks. On her father's insistence, Judith was permitted the title of queen. After Aethelwulf's death, however, the West Saxons reverted to custom. Alfred's wife Ealhswith was never called anything other than 'king's wife'; or later, when her husband died and her son Edward succeeded to the throne, 'king's mother'.[33]

Distrust of assertive female power underlies West Saxon attitudes to women in authority. The suspicion is evident in the legend of the wicked Queen Eadburh, said to be the last woman – with the exception of Judith of the Franks – to be permitted that title in Wessex. The tyrannical Eadburh (not to be confused with Aethelflaed's maternal grandmother of that name) had a short way with her enemies. She was ruthless towards anyone favoured by Beorhtric her husband.

Eadburh's tyranny, we are told, had lasting consequences in Wessex:

> *Not only did she earn hatred for herself, leading to her expulsion ... but she also brought the same foul stigma on all the queens who came after her. For as a result of her very great wickedness, all the inhabitants of the land swore that they would never permit any king to reign*

over them who during his lifetime invited the queen to sit
beside him on the royal throne.

It is no coincidence that Eadburh was the daughter of Offa, the feared Mercian king whose power threatened to overshadow that of Wessex in the late 770s. Peace was made between the kingdoms only when King Beorhtric acknowledged Offa as his overlord, and married Eadburh. Beorhtric's queen seems, at least in the legendary version, to have been regarded as a kind of fifth column within Wessex, an agent of the enemy capable of undermining the power and virility of the native royal line. That Eadburh's methods were said to be those of stealth – manipulation, slander and poison – reinforces this impression.

Eadburh's murderous career ended after she accidentally poisoned her husband the king, while trying to kill someone else. She fled abroad, to the court of Emperor Charlemagne, and the emperor is said to have given her a nunnery to administer. A few years later, however, she was expelled from her own convent for taking a lover. She ended up a beggar on the streets.[34]

No doubt Eadburh was held up to young Saxon princesses as a horrible example of what happens when women crave political power. This Wessex attitude, as will be seen, had persisted down the generations. It would have unfortunate implications in the course of time for the fate of Aethelflaed's only child.

Women in Wessex were expected to be wedded to domesticity, and not to stray too far from home. A set of maxims in the Exeter Book, a collection of Anglo-Saxon writings possessed by Exeter Cathedral, makes this clear: 'A woman who gads about attracts spiteful gossip; people accuse her; men speak scornfully about her; often her beauty wanes.'[35]

What the norms of a culture prescribe, however, and what maverick individuals opt to do about them, are often two different things. If Aethelflaed knew the Exeter maxims – and almost certainly she did, or some other version of them – a woman who would spend her adult life galloping about the country on horseback fighting Vikings and founding towns and churches, cannot have taken them too much to heart.

22

Religious traditions offered their own guidelines to high-status Anglo-Saxon women on what constituted feminine virtue. The church also regulated what occupations were, and were not, open to them. St Paul had taught that women should keep silent in the churches – a doctrine that, by the ninth century in Europe, wholly excluded them from the priesthood. Though ninth-century Anglo-Saxon women might hold power as heads of religious houses, even here the abbey or nunnery remained a foundation under royal (male) patronage. Abbesses were frequently in dispute with male kin who sought to reclaim monastic lands as their own.[36]

The highest ideal for a woman, according to church teaching, was lifelong virginity – or, failing that, constancy in marriage. One of the most positive things that could be said of a man's widow was that she remained 'chaste' after her husband's death. A virgin nun was, however, thought to be more pleasing to God than a widow (although it could be pointed out that the latter, given her supposedly lower spiritual status, might be less tempted to the sin of pride).[37]

Meanwhile men, at least in Anglo-Saxon royal families, engaged in serial monogamy; setting aside their wives to marry someone younger and more attractive, or who could offer a more useful political alliance through family connections. Some priests, as opposed to celibate monks, were married, but they, like their monastic brethren, still came out strongly for abstention from sexual relations as the highest ideal for women.[38] Anglo-Saxon legends of saints and nuns (largely composed by male clerics) dwell enthusiastically on examples of women who managed to retain their virginity from cradle to grave, like the holy nuns St Winifred, St Mildburh, or St Werburgh.

Running somewhat counter to the church's celebration of virginity, however, was the concept of the woman's function in marriage as a token of unity between two patriarchal dynasties; described in more idealised terms as that of a *frythwebba*, or 'peace-weaver'. Through such unions women could reconcile two peoples who had formerly been at war.

Her potential as a frythwebba was one reason to encourage a high-born woman to be a gracious hostess. The pre-Christian Anglo-Saxon tradition of dignified feminine hospitality continued in other forms in the Christian period, long after the old pagan mead hall as an institution had ceased to exist. The eleventh-century epic, *Beowulf* celebrates this bygone age:

> *Queen Wealhtheow plays the hostess.*
> *Consort of Hrothgar, of courtesy mindful,*
> *Gold-decked, greets the men in the building,*
> *And the freeborn woman the beaker presented.*
> *She offers the cup to her husband first,*
> *To the lord of the kingdom ... [39]*

The Exeter maxims offer a similar ideal of feminine social behaviour:

> *The woman shall prosper, beloved amongst her people.*
> *She shall be cheerful, keep a secret, shall be generous*
> *with horses and treasures. At the mead-banquet, always*
> *everywhere before the band of comrades, she shall greet*
> *the protector of the nobles first; quickly offer the first cup*
> *to the hand of the lord ... [40]*

A woman who sows discord and stirs up conflict in her community is censured. Like the wicked queen Eadburh, or like Thrytho, that other destructive legendary queen mentioned in *Beowulf*, a woman is condemned who constantly nurses resentment against others. Envy and hostility can make her 'a terror to all'. Everywhere in Anglo Saxon society, the ideal of 'peace-weaving' found its literal counterparts well beyond the idealised settings of heroic poetry, as ruling families swapped their female relatives in marriage for the sake of political alliances. Aethelflaed's aunt Aethelswith, Alfred's sister, as we have seen, was married off to king Burgred. Aethelflaed's own mother, the Mercian Ealhswith, in her wedding to Alfred was likewise married to draw together the always potentially antagonistic kingdoms of Mercia and Wessex. In this limited sense, the women were instrumental in 'making peace'; but their personal choice hardly came into it.

Now and again, there was a rebel. A case in point is Judith, daughter of the Frankish king Charles the Bald, who was married to Aethelflaed's grandfather Aethelwulf. Judith left the court of Wessex in 860, at least nine years before Aethelflaed was born. Her story, however, was so notorious, that it's hard to believe Aethelflaed could have been unaware of it as a family legend. Part of it was recorded by a scandalised Bishop Asser, in his biography of Aethelflaed's father.[41]

If Judith became the subject of scandal at the Wessex court, her career hardly began that way. She arrived in Wessex at the age of 14 – Alfred's father King Aethelwulf having picked her up as a bride in 856, on his way back from one of his Roman pilgrimages. Aethelwulf and King Charles, a powerful monarch who ruled over a territory roughly corresponding to modern France and Germany, shared concerns about the growing Viking threat, and saw the advantages of forming a defensive alliance. For Charles, the match was useful, too, to bring the prosperous kingdom of Wessex, a trade partner with the Franks, under his especial patronage. The bridegroom was marrying into the most famous and powerful European dynasty of the day. What Judith got out of the arrangement is harder to say. No one was likely to ask her how she felt about marrying a man several times her age and moving to a foreign country. Whether it was any consolation to her, that her father extracted the agreement allowing her to be called queen, is equally unknown.

Judith's childless marriage ended with the death of Aethelwulf two years later. She quickly became the wife of King Aethelbald, Aethelwulf's son.

The scandal of Judith's marriage to her stepson reverberated around Europe. It would have been endlessly discussed and deplored at the Wessex court, incurring 'great disgrace from all who heard of it'. Aethelbald, who seems to have been an unpopular ruler from the start, would have viewed the match as a means of consolidating his claim to the throne. Judith's opinion of the arrangement has, once again, gone unrecorded.

Two years later, this second royal husband also died; and the church declared Judith's second marriage illegitimate. With nothing to keep her in England any longer, the widow, now aged 18, sold the lands she had acquired in Wessex and went back home. Her father installed her at the monastery of Senlis in northern France, making clear that if she 'could not remain chaste', he would find a third husband for her. What he didn't expect was that Judith – probably having had enough of being handed round royal bridegrooms like a parcel – would choose a husband for herself. He was a nobody named Baldwin, and she ran off with him from the monastery. Predictably, King Charles was furious and refused to consent to the match. The matter came to the ears of the Pope, who, surprisingly perhaps, intervened on the side of Judith and Baldwin. The reluctant father-in-law made Baldwin respectable by naming him Count of Flanders, and gave him a parcel of land to defend against the Vikings. (Judith's son, Baldwin II, would later marry Aethelflaed's sister Aelfthryth. Peace-weaving indeed!)

Aethelflaed hardly needed to know people personally to be influenced by them. But if they were pointed out to her as moral examples, did she necessarily take from their story the lesson the narrator had intended? Judith's history might well have been held up to Aethelflaed as an example of precisely how a royal princess ought not to behave. What, however, if the future Lady of the Mercians viewed it instead as the narrative of a woman who, after suffering long enough at the hands of men, asserted her independence and made her own choices in the world?

The freedom of women in ninth-century Wessex was limited, certainly, especially before marriage. But we should not exaggerate the powerlessness of Aethelflaed and her sisters. For a start, women could own property. A minority of high-status West Saxon women owned quite a lot of it. Alfred left money to his closest female relatives in his will; though only one-fifth to each woman, of the £500 he left to each of his two surviving sons. It might appear, therefore, that the widow and the daughters were less valued than the king's male children. Or it might be that a man's financial burdens were likely to be greater than those of a woman, and that Alfred had taken this fact into account.

In addition to money, Alfred bequeathed estates to Ealhswith at Lambourn, Wantage and Edington. To Aethelflaed's younger sister Aethelgifu, abbess of Shaftesbury, he left Kingsclere and Preston Candover in Hampshire. Aelfthryth, the youngest, inherited land on the Isle of Wight, in Wiltshire and in Chippenham. To Aethelflaed, who by then was married to Aethelred of Mercia, he left the estate of Wellow in Hampshire, near the border with Wiltshire.[42] The female beneficiaries profited from these estates during their lifetimes, although the lands returned to the possession of their male kin after their deaths. All the same, wealth translated into a certain amount of independent power for aristocratic and royal women, especially as they were permitted to retain their property after marriage.

Women also held other people as property, as slaves. On rare occasions, they freed them. An ealdorman's wife in late tenth- or early eleventh-century Wessex (coincidentally named Aethelflaed) is recorded as freeing a slave named Aelfgyth in the presence of witnesses, 'for her soul and for the soul of her lord Ealdorman Aethelweard …'.[43]

One way in which high-status women could assert their independence, was by the founding and management of a nunnery. The age of dual-purpose monasteries, where a female abbess would rule over communities of both monks and nuns, was long gone, but a woman still could become head of a convent. These places afforded women a separate space, where it remained difficult for the male world wholly to impose its will.

Retiring to an abbey as her widowed mother before her had done, would have been the expected thing for Aethelflaed to do towards the end of her own life, after the death of Aethelred her husband; possibly leaving the rule of Mercia to her brother Edward. This was not Aethelflaed's way, however. Her choice was for an active life, out in the world. Why would she wish to exchange the role of Lady of the Mercians for that of abbess of some provincial convent? Both pagan and Christian traditions in Anglo-Saxon England emphasised that stoicism in suffering was a heroic virtue for women. (Anglo-Saxon women probably had to do quite a lot of it.) In poems and legends, women's heroism is seldom portrayed in terms of active initiative, but as a matter of courageous passive endurance. Everyone knew, for instance, the centuries-old legend of the martyred saint Juliana – how she endured torture and death, rather than marry the pagan husband chosen for her by unscrupulous male relatives. Boldly, Juliana tells her powerful and wicked suitor that if he will accept the Christian God, she will accept him as a husband – but on no other terms. The consequence of her refusal to marry, is martyrdom.[44]

The story preaches Christian steadfastness in the face of persecution. Did it also, perhaps, for a young Aethelflaed carry a second, less overt message – about the rightness of standing up to masculine oppression, at least if inflicted by pagans? That, after all, is what Aethelflaed went on to do for most of her adult life.

Surviving Anglo-Saxon literature offers two exceptions to the ideal of women as martyrs. One is the well-known poem 'Judith'. The story is taken from an apocryphal book of the Bible. Judith, a bold and clever woman, tricks her way into the enemy's camp and beheads the Assyrian chieftain Holofernes as he lies in his tent in a drunken stupor. Aided by her faithful handmaiden, Judith then returns to her people, and urges them to go forth and meet the Assyrians in battle, where the enemy is soundly defeated. Very much the central actor in this violent drama, Judith remembers to thank God for her achievement:

> *For all this, Judith spoke glory to the Lord of Hosts*
> *who had given her this honour, fame in the realm of earth,*
> *likewise reward in heaven, victorious recompense*
> *in the glory of the skies, because she had true belief*
> *always in the Almighty.*[45]

The poem 'Judith' may have existed during Aethelflaed's youth in Wessex, and been known to her. It may, however, not have been written until the early tenth century. Another active feminine role model, though – disturbing in some ways, inspiring in others – is suggested in Cynewulf's ninth-century poem, 'Elene', an Anglo-Saxon version of the Roman legend of Helena, and her finding of the True Cross. This may indeed have been one of the poems Aethelflaed memorised as a child. While there is much about it to offend modern sensibilities, it is interesting to speculate on what young Aethelflaed would have made of it, or of the story on which it is based, if she encountered the poem.

In Cynewulf's 'Elene', the Roman emperor Constantine orders his mother, 'The mighty queen / bold among the cities', to go to Palestine in search of the True Cross on which Christ was crucified. Elene arrives in Jerusalem at the head of an army. She accuses the Jewish inhabitants of Palestine of having betrayed Jesus to his death, and of having been cursed down the ages for their crime. (This is the notorious 'blood libel' that was to visit so many horrors on Jewish communities in Europe through the centuries.)

Elene then demands that the Jews of Palestine tell her where the True Cross is buried. They deny all knowledge of the matter. Elene calls them hard-hearted and obstinate. In a furious rant, she threatens them all with eternal damnation: 'A blazing pyre will grasp you on the hilltop, / the hottest of battle-flames ... will destroy / your raw flesh.' She takes prisoner an unfortunate man – stereotypically named Judas – and starves him in a pit. By this not-so-Christian method, she 'persuades' Judas to help her find the Cross. By divine inspiration, he is able to show her where it lies buried. The Cross then proves its genuineness by raising a dead man to life. After changing Judas's name to Cyriacus, Elene arranges for him to be made a bishop, and to found a new Christian community in Palestine. She returns in triumph to Rome, where nails from the True Cross are worked into a bridle for Constantine's horse – guaranteeing that Constantine will always be victorious in battle. Her son will have 'success at war, victory at strife, and peace everywhere'. The bridle will be 'famous throughout middle-earth ...'.[46]

Most striking, perhaps, in the portrayal of Elene is the image of her power. This queen is hardly the mild figure of the 'king's wife' or 'king's mother' of Wessex tradition, retreating into some convent in widowhood when her work in rearing the next generation of male rulers is done. Elene is an imposing figure, 'adorned in gold', and seated 'in majesty upon her throne'. She gives commands in an all-male world, and is obeyed. She constantly acts on her own initiative. She helps to found churches, and to bring people to the Christian faith. She retrieves holy relics and bestows them on her own people, to ensure their protection and prosperity.

To the modern understanding, the story of 'Elene' is replete with elements of bigotry, injustice and cruelty. Are these the elements, however, that in the relatively humane atmosphere of her parents' court, young Aethelflaed would have internalised? Or was there something else for her to take from the legend? Did the powerful image of Elene the Roman queen, majestic, authoritative, independent, a benefactor to her people, capture her imagination instead?

Beyond the encompassing world of women in which she spent her adolescent days, Aethelflaed would also have been aware of the world of men, with its boundaries and its roles sharply demarcated from those of women. The memory of her powerful paternal grandfather Aethelwulf, even though he had died before Aethelflaed was born, still hung around the court.

Her brothers, fathers, and male cousins talked constantly of battles past and fresh conflicts looming – of land management, tax revenues, endowment of churches, building projects, fortifications, court judgements, ecclesiastical appointments, hunting trips, and who was plotting against whom to gain the king's favour. If Aethelflaed was with her father at Athelney, she would already have witnessed some of this masculine world, at close quarters. And now at court, Alfred was constantly there, a tirelessly active presence – planning, discussing, ordering, instructing, and providing hospitality to visitors from far and wide.

Here, in the diverse multicultural environment, were more opportunities to observe and compare. There were diplomats from Flanders; refugees from Viking-occupied Mercia; a Viking who had become a Christian monk; Frankish and Irish scholars talking earnestly together in Latin. Young men from Gaul and the Scottish kingdoms, sent by their families to be trained up in Alfred's care. Sometimes wandering holy men would drop by, drawn by the king's reputation for piety and generosity, and Alfred would make them welcome.[47]

Amid this vibrant and ever-changing social scene, Aethelflaed could watch and listen, her astute practical mind consciously and unconsciously absorbing every detail of this male-dominated world. If it didn't immediately fascinate, if some of the talk of politics and finance didn't immediately make sense to her, here all the same was a wealth of vicarious experience to be stored away for later. In a future life, it would come into its own.

CHAPTER THREE

Marriage

'And know good counsel for them both as rulers together'. [48]

When Aethelflaed was about 15, her family decided it was time for her to have a husband. A bridegroom had been chosen for her – Aethelred, an *ealdorman* of Mercia.

In the church porch at Winchester, the couple exchanged their vows, surrounded by the members of their extended families, and the whole Wessex court. Afterwards, everyone crowded into the church to hear Mass, and the priests and choir chanting the Laudate Dominum.

This day marked the end of Aethelflaed's childhood, and of life with her family in Wessex. In a few days, she would follow her husband to his home across the border. Though she might not formally own the title for some years yet, her life as Lady of the Mercians had begun.

At first glance, it is difficult to see why Alfred chose Aethelred, an obscure ealdorman from Mercia, as a bridegroom for his eldest daughter, when he could have found her a husband among the Frankish princes, or even among her cousins in the royal house of Wessex. Alfred, however, knew what he was doing in his choice of this particular son-in-law. He needed a loyal, and preferably subordinate, ally in neighbouring Mercia, where the Viking-appointed puppet ruler Ceolwulf had died seven years before.

If Aethelred was not from the most distinguished royal family, he was hardly a menial either. In the strict hierarchical system of the ninth-century Anglo-Saxon world, an ealdorman held a rank just

32

below that of a king. In the royal court, he was normally a part of the king's inner circle; he often served as a high-ranking official, and would more or less automatically be a member of the king's *witan*, or council. An ealdorman would sometimes deputise for the king as a regional governor.[49] And Aethelred had promised to be loyal to King Alfred. A charter signed by Aethelred in 883 shows him acknowledging Alfred as his overlord.[50]

Aethelflaed's bridegroom was a member of the Hwicce tribe, whose leading family had once ruled over a small independent kingdom. The Hwicce had a power base in the area around Gloucester, until the kingdom was swallowed up in the larger political unit of Mercia. Aethelred may have been descended from an eighth-century Hwiccan ruler named Aethelmund, who is said to have founded the church at Deerhurst. Hwiccan royalty also built a mausoleum there. The Hwicce were known as patrons of Berkeley Abbey, thirty miles downstream from Deerhurst, along the banks of the Severn. These ancestral connections may well have motivated Aethelred to establish his main royal residence at nearby Gloucester.

How he spent the years when Mercia was under Viking control, and ruled by the Viking-appointed king Ceolwulf – especially given that during the winter of 877-8 the Vikings had an armed camp in his hometown – is a mystery. (The Vikings 'ravaged the kingdom of the Mercians,' we are told, before settling down in Gloucester.[51]) If Aethelred had been forced into exile during that time, there might well have been fellow feeling between himself and King Alfred, who had found himself in a similar predicament. Or possibly Aethelred had had some connection to Ceolwulf, and been under his protection?

In either case, Alfred had chosen Aethelred for practical reasons that looked to the future. The Wessex king not only gave Aethelred his daughter in marriage, but appointed the ealdorman to govern London, recently won back from Danish rule. This appointment, like the arranged marriage, was not just about Aethelred's social status, or even his Mercian ancestral connections, useful as they might be. It was about finding the right man for the job.

Alfred prided himself on his 'person skills', on knowing how to choose the appropriate human 'resources and tools'. A ruler must have 'praying men, fighting men and working men', he wrote. 'Without these tools no king may make his ability known.'[52] Like any competent modern human resources manager, he knew how to pick the most suitable person for a given role, and to make sure they did it to the best of their ability. He kept a careful eye on the functionaries in his kingdom, even local provincial judges or reeves. He sacked any he found incompetent or corrupt, or required them to undergo retraining.[53] When he wanted Latin religious texts translated into English, he assembled a team of scholars for the purpose. He probably commissioned the work of his biographer Asser, who has left posterity an eloquent account of the life of his employer – not, one imagines, without first receiving a nudge to undertake the work, from the royal elbow.

The king's immediate family, too, were co-opted into his managerial teams. Alfred chose his older son Edward, brave, ruthlessly practical and a quick decision maker, to lead his army, once Alfred became too old to do it himself. (An effective way, one would think, to prepare Edward for kingship after his father's death.) Aethelweard, Alfred's bookish younger son, who had been sent to formal schooling at an early age, may have gone into the church. The king's daughters, likewise, were assigned to positions deemed appropriate for them. Aethelgifu became the first abbess of Shaftesbury Abbey, an institution that lasted down the centuries until the Reformation. Aelfthryth was sent to consolidate Alfred's connections with Flanders through her marriage to Baldwin II. He would be a useful continental ally against the Vikings.

Aethelflaed was assigned the key role of cementing the ties between Wessex and Mercia. The connection would ensure Mercia remained subordinate to Wessex, while enabling King Alfred, and Edward after him, to keep a careful eye on what went on there.

It can hardly have failed to occur to Alfred that, in Aethelflaed's relationship with Aethelred, her social status as a royal princess and the Wessex king's eldest child, would give her something of an edge.

Even in a patriarchal social order, and in spite of her youth, Aethelflaed could claim rank over an ealdorman who had acknowledged Alfred as his overlord. No doubt this imbalance in the marital power relations suited Alfred well. It would prevent Aethelred getting inappropriate ideas about his position as ruler of Mercia, where he was Lord of the Mercians (*myrcna hlaford*) – not king.

When arranging this convenient match, Aethelflaed's father could hardly have anticipated that his daughter would outlive her husband to become Lady of the Mercians in her own right. Nor that she would lead armies into battle, or undertake the founding and re-modelling of Mercian towns. If Alfred knew his eldest daughter at all well, though, he would not have been too surprised.

As ruler of Mercia, King Alfred needed someone not only of the right social position, but someone with the qualities enabling him to hold on to power. For a governor of London, a place undergoing reconstruction after the Vikings had sacked it, a dependable person with integrity had been called for – practical, a good administrator. Alfred had judged Aethelred to be the man for that. Such qualities would equally be of use to Aethelred as lord of Mercia, but to maintain that second, higher position he would need to be tough as well. Almost every Anglo-Saxon ruler at some time faced a challenge to his right to rule, usually quite early on his tenure. If Aethelred wanted to remain Lord of the Mercians, as he had become before the end of Alfred's reign in Wessex, he would have to prove himself strong enough to keep the job, or not last very long.

What did Aethelflaed make of her bridegroom-to-be? We have no way of telling. Romantic historical novelists, in dealing with Aethelflaed's story, have been fond of making her out to be a reluctant bride, possibly yearning for an impossible liaison with some lovelorn suitor. The historical record offers not a scrap of evidence for any such romantic notions. Aethelflaed would certainly have expected to have a husband chosen for her by her family and would not have been surprised, or even displeased, to be married off to the Mercian ealdorman. Aethelred, likewise, had little choice in the matter – unless he wanted to insult the overlord who was ready to welcome him as a son-in-law.[54]

Aethelred would have been quite a lot older than Aethelflaed. She can have been no older than 16 when she married. But the bride's strong personality, as well as her royal status, went a long way to iron out the disparity. In any case, given the more enlightened attitudes to women's status that prevailed in Mercia, she was going to have more autonomy in this Mercian marriage than if she had been wedded to a member of the House of Wessex.

However much King Alfred might approve of him, Aethelred was not universally popular at the Wessex court. Bishop Asser, for one, didn't like him at all. Asser claims that as ruler in Mercia Aethelred oppressed the rulers of small Welsh kingdoms, who felt obliged to seek protection from King Alfred. Apparently, they preferred to have Alfred as their overlord to putting up with Mercian aggression:

'Hywel ap Rhys, [the king of Glywising], and Brochfael and Ffyrnfael [sons of Meurig and kings of Gwent], driven by the might and tyrannical behaviour of Ealdorman Aethelred and the Mercians, petitioned King Alfred … in order to obtain lordship and protection from him in the face of their enemies,' Asser writes.

Incidentally, in Asser's account we have a glimpse of the subordinate terms on which Aethelred himself had come under the rule of Wessex. Like the Welsh kings, in accepting King Alfred as his overlord, Aethelred too had promised that 'in every respect' he 'would be obedient to the royal will'.[55] Asser's account of the ealdorman's acceptance of Alfred as his overlord at least makes clear that Aethelred, who never styled himself 'king', but always 'Lord of the Mercians', fully accepted that Mercia was now politically subordinate to Wessex. All the same, there remained considerable ambiguity about his status as ruler – an ambiguity that would have troubling consequences for Aethelflaed and her adult daughter in the years to come.

That trouble, though, lay far in the future. For now, Aethelflaed's position as a princess of Wessex, wedded to Mercia's ruler while under her father's protection, looked secure indeed. One thing about Aethelred, that would have endeared him to his new in-laws, was that he very quickly distinguished himself in battle.

MARRIAGE

Aethelflaed and Aethelred had been married for about seven years when, in 892, Guthrum's successor as ruler in the eastern Danelaw, annulled the treaty Alfred had made with Guthrum by attacking Saxon lands in Kent, then Wessex. The relative peace of the previous fourteen years was shattered. Meanwhile, a new wave of Vikings, under the leadership of the fearsome warrior Haesten, arrived from continental Europe, raiding across Mercia from the Thames valley to beyond the River Severn in the west. That the invaders were finally held in check in Mercia was largely thanks to the heroic resistance of the Mercians and their Welsh allies, who had temporarily sunk their differences in order to resist the Vikings. The Mercian troops were led by Ealdorman Aethelred. He came from London the following year and joined Aethelflaed's brother prince Edward at the siege of Thorney Island, in Hertfordshire. When Edward's troops, for some unknown reason, gave up on the siege and went home, it was left to Aethelred to stay on and force the Vikings to surrender.

In spite of his defeat at Thorney, Haesten then took his army on a raid into southern Mercia. Aethelred, joined by Edward, attacked the Vikings at Benfleet, thirty-three miles east of London, on the northern bank of the Thames estuary. They killed many of Haesten's followers, and took as hostages Haesten's wife and sons.

That same year Aethelred mobilised a large force from across Southern Mercia, and besieged Haesten's army and his allies at Buttington, near Welshpool. When the Danes, who were starving, broke out of the siege and returned with reinforcements, he besieged them again at Chester, and they were forced to retreat into Wales. A new force of Vikings broke out from a Saxon siege at Hertford, and headed towards the northwest. Aethelred caught up with them at Bridgnorth, on the Severn, where he penned them in again.

The invaders had had enough. They gave up trying to gain any further foothold in Mercia for the time being, and went back east, to the Danelaw. When in 894 they again mounted a raid on Mercian territory, they took care to carry back their plunder through Viking-controlled Northumbria.

Sieges of Viking positions often ended inconclusively because Saxon conscripts became demoralised and went home. It might be that their required term of service had ended, but lack of food was another reason why Saxon armies voted with their feet. Aethelred made sure his soldiers had provisions enough to stay the course – and, one assumes, that they were regularly paid. He also could be ruthless, laying waste the Mercian farmland surrounding a siege, as he did at Chester – depriving the besieged Vikings of access to supplies, but also robbing local people of their livelihood. As a commander, however, it appears he considered the material needs of his followers, if only because it made sense militarily.[56]

These battles and sieges – mainly the latter – show a dogged, relentless quality in Aethelred, a capacity to stick it out till the bitter end. By the early 900s, however, while Aethelflaed was still only in her late twenties, it became apparent that her husband's stubborn courage to resist the Danes was increasingly being challenged. Not by Vikings, but by the failing capacities of his own body. Aethelred was becoming chronically ill.

This must in any case have been a sad time for Aethelflaed personally. Many of those back in Wessex whom she had looked to over the years for love, or for wise advice, were dying, or had gone far away. Her youngest sister Aelfthryth, married off to Count Baldwin, was now living in Flanders. Her aunt Aethelswith had died in 888 in distant Pavia and her younger sister, Aethelgifu, in 896, while still in her twenties. Aethelflaed's father died in 899, and her mother lived only a few years longer. Ealhswith's life ended in 902, at Nunnaminster, the abbey she had founded. Aethelflaed's maternal uncle, Ealdorman Aethelwulf, had died a year before his sister. Aethelwulf was a member of the Mercian court, and may have offered his niece valuable moral support during the first years of her marriage in Mercia. If so, he was no longer there for her to turn to.[57]

In Anglo-Saxon England, the last years of a century in any case usually carried with them a sense of apocalyptic foreboding. True, the end of the world was not expected until the year 1000. All the same, the late 800s and early 900s brought disturbing portents in the earth and heavens. In 896 there were epidemics in Wessex, 'with pestilence among cattle and men'. When Vikings gathered and built a settlement at Fulham on the Thames, that same year, 'the sun grew dark for one hour of the day'. In the autumn of 903, a comet appeared. In the following year the *Anglo-Saxon Chronicles* recorded an eclipse of the moon. The turn of the century must have seemed like a dark time indeed.[58]

Vikings were on the move again. In 902, a new Viking threat presented itself in Wessex, in an unexpected form. When Alfred died in 899, Aethelflaed's brother Edward had, as expected, succeeded his father as king of Wessex. However, one of his cousins decided to challenge Edward's right to the Wessex throne, claiming that he, Aethelwold, was the rightful heir.

Aethelwold was the son of Alfred's older brother, Aethelred. He had already tried once to overthrow Edward, but had been forced into exile in Northumbria. Now he was back, relying on the support of a Mercian ealdorman named Beorhtsige – plus a Danish fleet, and a force of Vikings recruited in East Anglia. They arrived from Essex, went deep into south-western Mercia, and very nearly got to Aethelred's base at Gloucester. Fortunately for the Mercians, however, the raiders veered southeast again, crossed the Thames and entered Wessex, to plunder Wiltshire. After Aethelwold was killed in battle in Kent, the rebellion petered out.

Mercia had been spared this time; but the vulnerability of Saxon communities to Viking attack had been exposed once more.

For Aethelflaed, her husband's illness meant growing responsibility. Now that Aethelred was unwell, she occasionally took major decisions. Increasingly, she acted as his deputy. The *Fragmentary Annals* tell us how in 902, seemingly on her own initiative, Aethelflaed granted lands to a community of Norwegians who had been driven out of Ireland:

> *Ingimund with his troops came to Aethelflaed, Queen of the Saxons; for her husband, Aethelred, was sick at that time. Now Ingimund was asking the Queen for lands in which he would settle, and on which he would build barns*

and dwellings, for he was tired of war ... Aethelflaed gave
him lands near Chester, and he stayed there for a time. [59]

Taking over from Aethelred in Mercia was not such a difficult transition for Aethelflaed. Even while her husband had been in better health, she and Aethelred had cooperated as equals in the government of Mercia, making many joint decisions.

In the late 890s and early 900s, Aethelflaed and Aethelred worked together tirelessly. Together they built defences against Viking incursions at Oxford, Hereford and Gloucester. Whether or not they knew it at the time, they had begun a work that would shape the face of the Midlands.

Aethelflaed already knew her role in this marriage. It would not be a subordinate one. Her place was beside her husband, shouldering with him the burdens of state. This, rather than bearing sons or founding and ruling a convent, like other royal women of her day, would be Aethelflaed's legacy to Mercia.

In 889, we find 20-year-old Aethelflaed joining her husband in witnessing a charter of her father's, a grant of waterfront property in London to her father's friend, Bishop Waerferth.[60] We see her already starting to work alongside Aethelred in ways that would one day prepare her to take on the business of ruling a kingdom by herself.

In the late 890s Aethelred and Aethelflaed jointly ordered the fortification of Worcester as a burh, a walled and heavily guarded town, its main streets laid out on a grid plan to afford swift access to the town walls in case of attack. Originally part of King Alfred's far-sighted scheme for a network of such fortifications to safeguard his people from Viking invasions, the burh at Worcester was just one of many projects Aethelflaed, with or without her husband, would undertake in Mercia.

A charter signed in Worcester records the plan to fortify the town, 'for the protection of all the people'. It provides for a grant of revenues, from taxes and collected fines, to Bishop Waerferth of Worcester, who had contributed money for building the new walls. It explicitly names both Aethelred and his wife as joint founders of the scheme: 'At the request of Bishop Wærferth, their friend, Ealdorman Æthelred and Æthelflæd ordered the burh of Worcester to be built …'. [61]

Another charter in Worcester, signed fourteen years after the plan to fortify the town, in recording a grant of land by Bishop Waerferth to Aethelred and Aethelflaed, not only names the beneficiaries jointly, but describes them jointly as rulers. They are both '*myrcna hlafordas*', 'lords of the Mercians', making clear that Aethelflaed, in ruling Mercia, is very much a partner with her husband.[62]

In a charter of 898, Aethelflaed is named – along with Plegmund, Archbishop of Canterbury, Bishop Waerferth, and Aethelred – as a member of a working group convened and overseen by King Alfred. The committee met to plan the rebuilding of London, still recovering from sacking and burning in the Viking raids and in need of new fortifications.[63]

Why Aethelflaed and Aethelred, in twenty-five years of marriage, had only one child – and a daughter at that – is a complete unknown. Normally a ruling couple would be anxious to have a male heir; a vital consideration in a society where women usually did not rule in their own right. Given the high rate of infant mortality, they would produce as many daughters as it took for a woman to finally give birth to a son. Aethelflaed's daughter Aelfwynn, however, remained an only child. It may be that Aethelred's illness, or the infertility of either husband or wife, was the cause of the unusually small family. The chronicler William of Malmesbury, writing in the twelfth century, has a different theory. He claims that Aethelflaed, 'from the difficulty experienced in her first (or rather only) labour, ever after refused the embraces of her husband, protesting that it was unbecoming the daughter of a king to give way to a delight, which after a time produced such painful consequences.'[64]

Where did William get this story? Did he simply make it up, to explain what, for a man of the twelfth century, might have otherwise seemed inexplicable – a woman producing only a single daughter? Aethelflaed may indeed have chosen to abstain from sex with her husband owing to the agony she suffered in giving birth to Aelfwynn. Or a painful first pregnancy could have made her physically unable to have another child. It is difficult, however, to imagine how William of Malmesbury could have known the facts of so personal a matter, a full two centuries after Aethelflaed's death.

In 910, fighting with the Danes flared up again. King Edward had recovered from a military setback in Wessex that had forced him to 'make peace' for a time with the Vikings, and was engaged in punitive raiding into the northern Danelaw. He raised a joint force of West Saxons and Mercians for a savage counter-attack on the Danelaw heartland that lasted five weeks, and 'very much harassed the northern army by … attacks on men and property'. The Danes would not suffer such an onslaught tamely. The scene was set for a showdown.

It happened in Mercia, at a place called Tettenhall – Wednesfield, near modern-day Wolverhampton. A large force of Vikings, on their way back from raiding across the Severn, found their route home to the Danelaw blocked by the Anglo-Saxon army, and were forced to fight for their lives. For them, the outcome was catastrophic. 'Many thousands' were said to have been killed, their leader, Eowils, among them.

In Mercia, the Danes never fully recovered from this shattering defeat. From now on they would find themselves on the defensive.[65]

Aethelflaed's husband must have been glad he had survived to witness the containment of his relentless enemy, and the respite gained for Mercia. The year after Tettenhall, he died. Aethelflaed had lost a husband and a co-worker – possibly, also, a friend. Now she would have to carry on alone.

CHAPTER FOUR

Remaking Mercia

'for the protection of all the people'.[66]

She sits watching from the end of the hall, enthroned above the tables, as the servants carry in loaded trays. Toasts are made, dignified speeches. Her guests settle down appreciatively to tackle the food. Cups are raised, guests drink health again to one another. The Lady smiles on them, part of her mind taking in the rich colours and patterns of the holiday clothes – noting who's here, who missing from the feast this Easter. The feast of a resurrection to life, and life must go on. Always, though, for her the lurking sense of an absence – of one who for so long was always beside her, a sturdy pillar holding up her world.

An elderly thegn comes up and greets her respectfully. Her late husband knew him well. She smiles and says something kindly and polite, seeing the condolence in his eyes. It is the end of a partnership that lasted a quarter of a century. Aethelflaed now finds herself a widow, no longer young, and sole ruler of Mercia. To the Mercians, or at least to those of them able to topple her from power if they so choose, she will now have to prove her ability to rule without Aethelred to guide her. In spite of Aethelflaed's evident capacity to defend her realm, and her long track record of working to make it peaceful and prosperous, there will always be a few ambitious contenders willing to replace her if ever she should falter. There are mutterings in some quarters, about the impropriety of a woman ruling alone without a husband. Nothing like it has been seen in Anglo-Saxon England before. Still, she is known and trusted for her long track record of work with Aethelred. And most of her ordinary subjects would prefer continuity to the chaos a succession conflict would unleash.

Her Mercian maternal ancestry is helpful to her. Like many people brought up with parents from different backgrounds, Aethelflaed is 'bilingual' – able to assume a Mercian accent and use Mercian dialect words when she chooses. It is a great asset when she gives a rousing speech to her soldiers before a fight, or when haranguing some unfortunate builder who has failed to complete work on time.

She has strong supporters and capable advisers. Her thegns follow her loyally into battle. In the church, she can turn for both spiritual and legal or political counsel, to Archbishop Waerferth of Worcester, an old friend of her father.

Her brother, King Edward of Wessex, is another matter. While he surely would welcome the stability guaranteed by his sister's continuing rule, and is glad to keep the always potentially volatile situation in Mercia under the watchful eye of a close relative, he will remain concerned that the ruler of the sub-kingdom might grow too independent. Provided Aethelflaed accepts that Mercia remains subject to the final jurisdiction of Wessex, he will work with her.

Edward has already made one decision, however, that has the effect of cutting Aethelflaed, and Mercia, sharply down to size. She had scarcely begun her unilateral reign as Lady of the Mercians, when he had her cede to him, and to Wessex, a large chunk of Mercian territory in the southeast. It is hard to believe she has given up this sizable swathe of her kingdom – fully one quarter of its total area – without reluctance, not least because the arrangement deprives Mercia of access to the Thames, and the wealthy continental trade based in London.[67]

There is plenty more to keep her on her guard. There are, once again, Vikings at the gate. The Danish kingdom of York has been decisively weakened by recent Saxon victories; but there are always roving bands of opportunists riding out of Leicester, or others crossing into Mercia from Wales. These adventurers will certainly see her husband's death as an opportunity. Not that Aethelflaed has the reputation of a weakling. She has already commanded troops in battle and repelled invaders, an indispensable qualification for any Mercian ruler in these times. She may even have fought beside her brother in 910, when joint West Saxon and Mercian forces turned the tide at the battle of Tettenhall.

It is sometimes suggested that wounds received at Tettenhall were the cause of Aethelred's death. But he clearly had been chronically ill for a long time before that. It is unlikely that by 910, the year before his death, he would have been able to go out and fight. It's quite possible, therefore, that it was Aethelflaed who led the Mercians at Tettenhall. And three years earlier, she had directed the defence of the town of Chester against Norwegian Vikings and their allies.

Aethelflaed had granted lands near Chester to the Norsemen who had been driven out of Ireland, probably in the expectation that they would defend the Wirral against attacks by Danes from York. For a few years, the plan seemed to work well. By 907, however, the Norsemen, under their leader Ingimund, had grown dissatisfied with an apparently generous arrangement. They had their eyes on a bigger prize – the prosperous town of Chester, with its markets and royal court centre, its access to navigation and the waterfront trade of the River Dee. Ingimund, it is said, began 'complaining bitterly'. He said they were 'not well off unless they had good lands', and that they should seize control of Chester. 'Let us entreat and implore them ourselves first,' he urged, 'and if we do not get good lands willingly like that, let us fight for them by force.' Ingimund enlisted some Danes as his allies, and 'All the chieftains of the Norwegians and Danes consented' to his plan.[68] While some details of this story have been questioned, in its essentials it has a ring of truth about it. It is altogether plausible that after a few years Ingimund and his followers would grow restless with the deal Aethelflaed had offered them. It is also unlikely that Aethelflaed, determined, resourceful and quick-thinking, would allow one of her major town centres, in a strategic location, to be seized by Vikings without putting up a fight.

Even while Ingimund was raising his joint Norwegian and Danish force to attack Chester, Aethelflaed became aware of his plans. Mobilising an army of her own, she 'filled the city of Chester with her troops'. By the time the Vikings arrived at the gates of Chester, the whole army, 'with many freemen', was waiting for them inside the town walls.

Aethelflaed then set a trap. She sent a smaller force outside the walls to fight with the Vikings. Her men would stage a retreat into the town, 'as if defeated', so that a second force, of soldiers on horseback, could ambush the invaders once they got inside and the gates were closed to prevent their escape. 'Everything was done accordingly', the chronicler tells us, 'and the Danes and Norwegians were frightfully slaughtered in that way.' But the survivors left outside the town gates, hardened Viking warriors that they were, fought on, refusing to surrender. They began trying to breach the town wall, using wooden props as supports in the gap they made.

Aethelflaed sent messengers to some Irishmen who were with the Viking attackers, reminding them of past goodwill between Irish and Saxons, and calling on them to entrap the Danes. The Irish should ask the Danes to promise rewards for betraying the city into their hands. When the men laid down their weapons, to swear an oath on their shields, the Irish would attack and kill them. 'All this was done accordingly ...'.

The besieged residents of Chester, meanwhile, dealt with the Norwegians, who were still busy trying to hammer their way through the town wall. The defenders threw down rocks and followed up with boiling liquids, poured down from cauldrons onto the attackers below, 'so that their skin peeled off them'. When the Norsemen tried to shield themselves from the scalding downpour, fashioning overhead canopies out of animal skins, the defenders are said to have dropped their beehives on the attackers, 'which prevented them from moving their feet and hands because of the number of bees stinging them'. This biological warfare was finally too much for the Vikings. They 'gave up the city', and left.[69]

Clutching at her horse's reins, very still, she looks down from a hillock on her troops, a dark mass bristling with spears – all she can see of them from this height. She raises her right arm – the signal they've been waiting for. The mass spreads forward. Riding down towards them, she sees them break into a clumsy run, the thick grass clogging their feet. A collective roar breaks from their throats, the cry of a hunting beast as it brings down the kill. The enemy are in sight. If Aethelflaed's heart beats faster, if she tenses and sweats – realises with a sinking in her stomach that her army is heavily outnumbered, her face remains impassive. She knows her troops are battle-hardened, disciplined and brave. The Vikings, however many they are, look like a rabble. So she tells herself.

She watches tensely as, with another roar, then a sickening crash, the two armies collide, the warriors of the front line battering against the opposing row of shields. Aethelflaed's horse stirs nervously under her. She reins it in – forces herself to stay put. Her every nerve taut, her brain racing, thinking ahead. If they can drive the Vikings off the field, where will the enemy go? To hole up somewhere, no doubt. In the wood she can see from here, looming darkly over the valley? Or can her troops chase them up to there? Box them in? If, of course, the battle goes the other way, they may all shortly be fighting for their lives.

Where, and how, did Aethelflaed learn to handle weapons? It was hardly part of the curriculum for a young female growing up in ninth-century Wessex. If West Saxon women were not expected to rule, they certainly were not expected to fight.

A few people have tried to answer this question. The historical novelist Rebecca Tingle has invented a story where young Aethelflaed has a guardian before marriage, who teaches his charge combat techniques in secret. Aethelflaed could equally have learned by watching her male relatives, or the thegns at her father's court, as they trained and practised swordplay, and copying their moves. Later in life, she would have been free to engage some young warrior to coach her. But then other questions arise. Saxon-Viking warfare was heavily physical, dependent not just on courage, but on muscle strength and stamina. Can we really imagine the Lady of the Mercians, whose life as a royal princess would hardly have trained her as an athlete, slugging it out with large brawny warriors on the battlefield? Did she ever kill anyone with her own hands? It's likely that she went to war on a horse, which would have given her an advantage over any man fighting on foot; except that the Viking leaders would themselves have been mounted, and Aethelflaed, even with her face hidden by a helmet, would have been a visible target to them.

One historian portrays Aethelflaed, after a victory, striding (or strolling), onto the scene as the Danes are about to surrender. Presumably, in this historian's image of the event, she has given orders to her troops, then stood and watched the ensuing battle from a safe vantage point in the rear of the fighting.[70]

Anglo-Saxon battle was not a subtle affair. The main tactics were two – the siege, and the shield wall. On the open battlefield, the opposing armies would march towards one another, uttering war cries and banging on their heavy shields with the flat of their swords to intimidate the enemy. As they closed together, those in the front line locked their overlapping shields together to form a solid wall. The two armies then clashed together, striking at one another with their swords, while those behind them hurled spears into the enemy ranks. Once the ranks of the weaker side collapsed under this assault, the fighting would be chaotic and bloody; hand-to-hand combat, leaving men either dead or maimed, groaning in agony.

All warfare is barbaric, and Saxons and Vikings were not acquainted with the Geneva Conventions. Fighting might rage for hours, but sooner or later the nerve of one side or the other would break and, in a collective stampede, the whole army would turn and flee. The victors would then pursue the fugitives, cutting them down from behind as they ran.

The *Fragmentary Annals of Ireland* tell of Aethelflaed's involvement in 'a hard and ferocious' fight with 'dark and fair foreigners' on the Danelaw border, with many killed on both sides. The chronicle account clearly contains a large dose of legend. After, we are told, the Vikings had been put to flight, the Viking leader was taken ill. He 'was carried out of the battle to a forest nearby, and he died there'. Another leader, Oittir, 'when he saw the Saxons slaughtering his people, fled into a dense wood near him, along with those of his people who survived'. The Mercian army – 'a huge throng' – pursued the fleeing Vikings and surrounded the wood. Aethelflaed then 'commanded them to hack down all of the forest with their swords and battleaxes'. Deprived of their hiding place, 'the pagans were slaughtered'. After this bloody victory, Aethelflaed's fame, it is said, 'spread in all directions'.[71]

Oittir is the Norse leader who was killed at the Battle of Corbridge, on the River Tyne, in 914 or 918. If we take the earlier battle date, it is just possible that Aethelflaed was there, having led her troops over 120 miles northward across the Danelaw border, then forty miles to the east through Northumbria. She could have gone to support her Scots allies, who were then struggling to resist Danish and Norse aggression.

The tree-cutting story, though, certainly needs to be treated with scepticism. Even if the Mercians had the Vikings surrounded, it would take quite a long time to cut down a whole wood. Besides, it would not do much good to the edge of anyone's sword to use it for hacking at trees. The Mercians would have been more likely to besiege the cornered Vikings until hunger drove them to surrender or try and fight their way out – that was the usual Anglo-Saxon tactic in such situations. Still, the Irish story makes the valid general point: this was a woman who was more than a match for Vikings.

For the next five years of her reign, Aethelflaed had no need to take to the battlefield. She was able to turn to more constructive work. In conjunction with her brother in Wessex to the south, she was engaged in the ongoing project that had begun in the early years of her marriage, and been carried on through the time of her husband's last illness. Less obviously dramatic than her heroic and violent deeds in battle in defence of lands and lives – the actions that have most captured the imagination of historians – was the important work of building the burhs, a network of forts and fortified towns across the Midlands. From Hereford to Warwick, Oxford to Chester, these massive defences not only kept her people safe from attack, but brought prosperity to Mercia and changed the face of the region in ways that resonate even to the present day.

If she had put her own life on the line in her battles with the Viking invaders, she took an equally personal and direct interest in the construction of defences to keep them out. Almost certainly, she herself chose the location of each new fortified town. She did so with an eye to its strategic location, sited on a hill, or protected by a bend in a river. Probably she sometimes oversaw the progress of the actual construction herself. One can picture her riding slowly around a partly-built earthen rampart, reining in now and again to inspect the work closely. Summoning a foreman to her, to point out an expanse of crumbling soil beside a gate, that would give way at the first heavy rain; or querying some delay in delivering timber for the palisade.

A typical burh was built on a stone foundation, with earthen ramparts and ditches encircling the site. On this basic foundation a wooden palisade was built, set at intervals with heavy wooden posts carved from the trunks of trees. Or where, as at Gloucester and Chester, Roman defences had left stone walls, these might be brought back into use. Inside the burh walls ran walkways at different heights, with watchtowers above them.

The burh could be a lone outpost – a fort guarding some strategic location, or it could encompass a whole town. Whether large or small, the basic pattern was a simple one. Within the encircling protective wall, central streets were laid out in a cross, often with smaller streets running off them in a grid pattern. To allow easy access to the outer defences in case of attack, a smooth road was built, running round the inside perimeter of the burh wall.

Each burh, whether a simple fortress overlooking some bridge or valley vulnerable to Viking incursions, or a whole fortified town, was capable of functioning as a single defensive unit. The walls were manned by guards conscripted from the locality who had every interest in defending their native patch of land. From every 'hide' – a hide being an area of land capable of supporting one extended family – a guard would be recruited, until there were enough to have a man stationed every four yards along the perimeter wall. (The accuracy with which this prescription was followed is suggested by excavations at Worcester, where one shift of the town's garrison was said to have drawn on recruits from 1,200 hides of land to cover approximately 4,950ft of wall. An estimated measurement of the Worcester town walls came up with a figure of 4,650ft.)[72] The guards were well trained and armed, and received payment raised from the local community. Each contingent of soldiers served a prescribed term of service, before a new garrison would relieve them. It is possible that some of the guards were given 'burgage' plots in new burh towns, enabling them to build themselves homes, grow market gardens, set up small businesses, and generally settle down as town dwellers.[73]

In time, the burhs would form a protective grid in which each fortified place lay no more than thirty or forty miles from the next, making it increasingly difficult for Viking raiders to rampage unchecked through Saxon territory. And safety bred prosperity. Out of isolated, vulnerable hamlets, now securely ringed with walls and guarded day and night, emerged thriving market towns, with streets laid out in an orderly grid pattern – embryos of principal towns of the Midlands we know today.

As we have seen, Aethelflaed and Aethelred worked together on the founding of burhs during the early days of their marriage. The founding of the new town of 'Oxnaford' or Oxford, conveniently located halfway between Worcester and London, with its neat grid of streets inside its protective wall, is said to have been commissioned by Aethelflaed during her husband's lifetime, in the years before she ceded that part of Mercia to Edward.[74]

Some time between 901 and 912, the Mercian rulers founded another new fortified town – Shrewsbury in Shropshire, to keep watch from a hilltop over a bend in the Severn. The river encircles the base of the hill, almost making of it an island. With its long-range view of the valley below, the site must have struck Aethelflaed as perfect for building the new burh. The church she ordered built at the town's highest point could also have served as a lookout, giving local people outside the burh time to come in and take shelter in the event of an attack. Shrewsbury prospered in the long run, becoming Shropshire's county town, with a population of 100,000 today.

The towns that Aethelflaed and her husband restored, expanded and fortified at Worcester, Hereford and Gloucester each guarded a major river, with Hereford on the Wye, Worcester on the Severn, and Gloucester downstream to the south. The three towns together, less than thirty miles from one another, formed a protective triangle for the mutual defence of all.

Gloucester was of particular importance to Aethelred, as the place that would become his royal capital in the south of Mercia. His roots went deep in the town. His forebears had founded a church in Gloucester, and a monastery for monks and nuns, ruled over by a Hwiccan princess. Here, the Mercian witan would meet, and here the Lord and Lady of the Mercians would establish their residence, half a mile outside the town limits, at Kingsholm.

Before the town as a whole could become fit for purpose, however, a great deal of work had to be done. After the last Roman legions had left Britain, Gloucester – once the noble Roman *colonia* of Glevum, had gradually fallen into disrepair. The fine stone buildings – the baths and colonnades, the stone-built houses, and even the very city walls – crumbled and fell. The city's residents began to build wattle and daub houses in place of stone ones, and established smallholdings among the ruins, where dung heaps grew up beside living quarters, and the main thoroughfares filled with hillocks of rubble. The Viking occupation during the winter of 877-8 can hardly have improved matters. If nothing else, it would have decimated the local population. Gloucester had effectively ceased to function as an urban centre and had become a semi-rural slum. Aethelred and Aethelflaed saw that radical measures were needed.

One of the most dramatic was moving the line of the city's defences to follow the waterfront, a move that at once almost doubled the town's available land area. It gave easier access to the banks of the River Severn, which at that time flowed close to the west end of the city. A bridge over the river led to open countryside, enabling farmers to bring in their produce for sale. The Severn, with its abundance of fish, its banks thick with reeds and willows that could be used for thatching roofs and to make baskets, mats and furniture was in itself a rich commercial resource. The waterfront facilitated commerce, enabling goods to be brought into Gloucester from as far away as Ireland, and locally made products to be shipped out. The riverside would also be the chosen location for the new and beautiful church of St Peter (later St Oswald's), which Aethelflaed and her husband would later found.

The couple ordered the rebuilding of the town walls, and its gates to the east, south and north. They oversaw reconstruction of the town's central Market Cross, with its four streets running to the gates in each direction of the compass. New markets were established. The town was once again able to grow.

Trade and manufacturing in the city quickly began to recover. The town's mint was turning out coins, there was metalworking and a pottery industry. The reconstruction of Gloucester was about more than simply building military defences to protect the population – though it was that, too. It was a work of revival – bringing a dying urban community back to life.

In 907, after her husband became ill, it fell to Aethelflaed to restore the old Roman walls at Chester. The town – its very name derived from the Latin word 'castrum', for 'camp', which went into Anglo-Saxon as 'ceastre' – had been of key strategic importance to the Romans. The town's position on the Dee made it a lucrative trading centre – as we have seen, it was a tempting prize for Viking invaders for this reason. It was important to the rulers of Mercia, too, for its closeness to the Welsh border, with the ever-present potential for clashes between Celts and Saxons.

At Chester, large stretches of the Roman wall remained intact. Where they had fallen, Aethelflaed rebuilt them. She ordered the rubble cleared from the town centre, and, as she had at Gloucester, rebuilt the central streets at right angles where they had been pushed awry by the accumulation of giant heaps of debris. Chester's burh took the shape of an oblong, a quarter of a mile across from west to east, with half a mile of streets and buildings stretching down to the river. Walled on three sides, the burh's southern wall gave onto the Dee.

(As at Gloucester, the river, that defensive barrier and lifeline, flowed closer to the town than it does nowadays.)

Under Aethelflaed's rule, Chester became a safe space for many ethnic groups – Scandinavian settlers and merchants, Welsh and Irish, Franks, Scots and Saxons – who came together to manufacture and to trade.

Three years later, she founded a fort at 'Bremesbyrig' – thought to be either Bromsberrow in Gloucestershire, or Bromesberrow near Ledbury in Herefordshire. In either situation, a burh would afford effective protection for both Hereford and Gloucester. Two years later, she expanded that protection by building at a strategic crossing point of the River Severn, at Scergeat, making it difficult for Vikings to move freely in and out of Wales and the Welsh borders. With characteristic thoroughness, she went to survey the site in person: 'Here, on the holy eve of the Invention of the Holy Cross [May 2], Aethelflaed, Lady of the Mercians, came to Scergeat and built a stronghold there.'

It was later that same year, according to the *Anglo-Saxon Chronicles*, that she oversaw the building of a burh at Bridgnorth. Like the burh she had established at Shrewsbury, this was a new town on a hill overlooking the Severn, with a church keeping watch over the river valley from its highest point. The hill and river together provided a formidable defensive system; and there is a panoramic view from the hilltop across the valley below. The new burh was the embryo of the small Shropshire community (population 12,000) that exists today. In 896, the Danes had wintered by the Severn in the Bridgnorth area. They would find it impossible to do so again.[75]

Tamworth, the royal centre in the north of Mercia, less than a day's ride from the Danelaw border, was a place in obvious need of protection. It came next on Aethelflaed's itinerary, after she had secured the line of defence along the Severn. The palace on a hill, overlooking the junction of the Tame and Anker rivers, was in a state of ruin after the Viking raids – and presumably, the warfare that had finally driven the Vikings from that part of Mercia. In 913, according to the *Anglo-Saxon Chronicles*, 'God helping, Aethelflaed, Lady of the Mercians, went … to Tamworth, and then built the stronghold there.' Her whole court – 'all the Mercians' – accompanied her. As a practical 'hands-on' ruler, she would have ridden around the site of the projected new town to assess the most effective way of building its defences, and overseen the final plans herself. Aethelflaed had the palace rebuilt inside the new town walls. The burh had three gates in the northern, western and eastern walls, and a bridge on the fourth side that gave access to the River Tame. She surrounded the whole structure with a sturdy palisade – the posts in the palisade were cut from massive tree trunks two feet in diameter – and with an outer bank and ditch that together measured 28ft across.[76]

At Stafford, later that summer, Aethelflaed founded another new town. She selected as its site a half-mile-long islet, little more than a sandbar, cradled on three sides by a bend in the River Sow, and protected to the north by marshland. As she chose this place, did her father's refuge on the marsh-encircled island of Athelney come to mind? Like Athelney, this place too had sacred associations. Saint Bertelin was said to have founded the church there in the eighth century, and the place was still home to a small religious community. Soon the quiet would be broken by the clamour of hammers and axes, as workmen felled trees and carted their trunks over makeshift bridges, for the building of sturdy wooden walls atop the newly dug earthen ramparts. New streets were laid. One of these, running north to south (and now known as Greengate Street), possibly followed an existing track across the width of the islet. A slightly irregular 'cross' of streets intersected this main thoroughfare, where a market was established. These secondary streets, running east and west would, when the town was first built, have extended as far as the burh walls rather than ending in a market square and a churchyard respectively, as they do now.

Manufacturing and large-scale food production quickly developed in the town. Grain was milled, animals butchered for meat. There was a forge for metalworking that made weapons, and an industrial kiln for the production of a distinctive orange-coloured pottery, named by late twentieth-century archaeologists, 'Stafford Ware'. In late medieval times, Stafford would emerge as a centre of the wool trade.[77] The founding of the new town protected a vulnerable rural population and made for greater security generally, in an area uncomfortably close to Danish territory. Fortifying Stafford also shielded the important bishopric of Lichfield from Viking-occupied Leicester and Derby, and guarded a strategic crossing point on the Tame.

The following summer, a fort was built at Eddisbury, to the south east of Chester, squarely in the centre of northern Mercia, with Runcorn to the north. It has been suggested that this was an abortive effort to build a burh in the wrong place. It could equally, however, have been designed as backup for Chester and Runcorn – burhs that watched over the two great waterways of Dee and Mersey – to guard against attack from the east.

A crucial spot many miles to the south, still closer to the Danelaw border, was Warwick. Founding a new town here provided a further shield for already-fortified Worcester, and increased protection for Gloucester. Aethelflaed had the burh built there, that summer of 914, 'late in harvest-time'. (What the conscripted labourers who worked on the huge burh would have thought about being taken away from their fields at the busiest time of the farming year is not recorded. One would like to know whether they cursed, or whether they resigned themselves to doing the job, reflecting that it was all for the common good.)[78]

Observing the occasional reluctance of the people to respond to King Alfred's orders to build the early burhs in Wessex, Bishop Asser had little sympathy for the tragedies that befell those who disobeyed the royal command. If work on a burh was left undone, 'because of the people's laziness', and it was 'not finished in time to be of use' to those working on it, local people could be massacred or enslaved in a Viking attack. What then, was the use of 'meaningless repentance', Asser demanded, after a community had been reduced to 'virtual extinction' for lack of adequate defences? The *Anglo-Saxon Chronicles* give a graphic account of what could happen if a burh was not completed to order. In Kent in 892, when Vikings came up-river, they were able to destroy an incomplete fort near the Thames, and then to ravage the area as they pleased: 'Inside that fortress sat a few peasant men, and it was half-made.'[79]

One major advantage of the burh system, was that it made the citizens of each locality responsible for, and self-sufficient in, their own defence. By 914 this self-sufficiency was starting to prove its worth. In that year, an army of Vikings came up the Severn, raiding across Wales. They tried to move eastwards into Mercia, and set out to attack Archenfield in Herefordshire, but encountered unexpected local resistance: 'They were met by the men from Hereford and from Gloucester and from the nearest strongholds', who 'fought against them and put them to flight'. The men from the burhs killed Hroald, the Viking leader, and 'a great part of the raiding-army'. They cornered the Viking force in an 'enclosure', and 'besieged them there until they gave them hostages, that they would leave King Edward's domain'. The residents of the area did not have to summon an entire army to their defence. They were now capable of warding off attackers by themselves.[80]

By late in the winter of 915, Chirbury in Shropshire had a new basic fortress, a simple structure of banks and ditches. Aethelflaed moved on to 'Weardbyrig' – a place whose whereabouts is lost to history. (One possibility is Warburton in Cheshire, on the south bank of the Mersey.) She built a third burh in 915, at Runcorn in Cheshire. The ditch on the landward side of this burh was cut into solid rock. With a commanding view over the Mersey Narrows, watchmen here could keep a lookout for unfriendly shipping coming from Ireland, and a careful eye on the traffic between the two Viking bases of Dublin and York.[81]

Aethelflaed may, as local tradition claims, have founded a burh at Wednesbury, near Wolverhampton; although the evidence for this is inconclusive. The summit of Church Hill, once sacred to Woden, would have certainly made a safe defensive position, affording views for several miles in all directions.[82]

Chester and Bremesbyrig, Scergeat and Bridgnorth, Tamworth, Stafford, Eddisbury, Warwick, Chirbury, Weardbyrig, Runcorn … Between 907 and the spring of 916, Aethelflaed had constructed a formidable grid of defences across the length and breadth of Mercia. Her brother Edward, meanwhile, had embarked on a similar task for Wessex, with forts at Hertford, Buckingham, Towcester, and later all over the heartland of the reconquered eastern Danelaw. Of the roughly twenty-two burhs built over a twenty-year period, however, a dozen of them at least were the sole work of the Lady of the Mercians. Several places – notably Gloucester and Chester, had to be rebuilt from a state of ruin. Tamworth was expanded from the site of a royal residence to a new urban centre. At least five sites – Stafford, Warwick, Bridgnorth, Runcorn and Shrewsbury – saw the founding of entirely new towns from scratch.

Aethelflaed's building programme was nothing if not systematic. She worked steadily around her kingdom, securing and rebuilding the towns in the south, then constructing forts on the Welsh borders, and guarding the crucial trade route of the Dee at Chester. Next, she reinforced and expanded the ancient palace complex at Tamworth, laying out new streets there, and built at Stafford and Warwick, to afford further protection from the Danelaw. Finally, the fortified town at Runcorn was founded, to keep watch over the great northern waterway of the Mersey.

While the burh system was highly effective in protecting the population and preventing Viking raids across most of Mercia, it could not be infallible. Tamworth, in particular, long remained a border town with the Danelaw, ever vulnerable to attack. In 943, twenty-five years after Aethelflaed's death, a Viking raiding party succeeded in burning down the church. Yet in spite of this setback, the safety and prosperity that Aethelflaed's building programme brought to Mercia as a whole, is undeniable.

In 916, when her burhs had secured the heartland of Mercia, Aethelflaed went to war again – this time on a punitive expedition against 'Brecon Mere', the kingdom of Llangorse in southern Wales. She 'sent an army' that raided and destroyed a fortified island town on a lake at the heart of the small Welsh community, and brought back to Mercia the queen of Brecon Mere and thirty-three others as hostages.[83]

The immediate trigger (or possibly the pretext) for this action was the murder on 16 June of an abbot named Ecgbert, 'guiltless ... killed with his companions'. They were all perhaps members of some small monastic community, attacked in search of plunder. As if to emphasis Ecgbert's status as a martyr, the *Anglo-Saxon Chronicles* give the day of the abbot's death as the feast of St Cyricus, a child saint killed by pagans in the fourth century. The allusion suggests that whoever killed the abbot and his companions, were pagans too. A man murdered by fellow Christians might be thought of as a victim, certainly, but hardly as a martyr.

Why did Aethelflaed care so deeply about the killing of this one man, that after only three days, she dispatched an avenging army? The clue, if we believe the Welsh chronicler Caradoc, lies with the ruler of Brecon Mere.[84] Trewyr was a Viking who had married a Welsh princess, in order to settle on her land. He seems to have been gathering other Viking colonists around him. Were these settler Vikings starting to present a threat to Mercia, not unlike that posed by Ingimund's people in Chester, nine years before?

It would not be the last time that conflict with the Vikings was complicated by an involvement from Wales. Caradoc tells us that when Aethelflaed attacked the Danish-held town of Derby in the summer of 917, she was pursuing a Welsh leader named Huganus, who had raided into Mercia, and then fled to the Danelaw.[85] When she took Derby, she caught up with Huganus, who, 'perceiving himself to be over-matched, chose rather to fall by the sword, than cowardly to yield himself to a woman'. The Huganus story suggests that Aethelflaed was continuing to have problems with raiders into Mercia from across the Welsh border.

She no doubt had more important reasons to attack Derby, however, than to pursue a stray Welsh bandit. From Derby to Tamworth is less than thirty miles. An army of raiding (or invading) Danes on horseback could have covered that distance in under a day. Aethelflaed, child of a Mercian mother, would have been familiar with the grim story of Repton, only nine miles south of Derby, where, in the winter of 873-4, Vikings had smashed and plundered the royal mausoleum, and incorporated the abbey building into their new fortress. Her own childhood memories of how Vikings had descended on Chippenham from Gloucester – also over a distance of thirty miles – would have made her even more conscious of the threat the Danes in Derby might pose to Tamworth.

It was not as if the Vikings had settled down quietly to mind their own business in the Danelaw. Even though the Danish kingdom at York was by now solidly established, there would always be some maverick band of adventurers ready to seek their fortunes by plundering Anglo-Saxon lands. The year 917 was one of raids out of Northampton, 'and from Leicester and north of there' into eastern Wessex. Danish forces attacked Towcester, near Buckingham, then Bedford. The men of Bedford resisted, and put the Vikings to flight. Then the raiders were into Mercia, crossing the kingdom as far as Herefordshire, where they besieged the fortress at 'Wigingamere' (Wigmore). (Here, although the attackers fought 'long into the day' and made off with cattle from the surrounding countryside, once again a well-guarded burh proved its ability to protect the people sheltered inside.[86])

All through that year, fighting raged across eastern Wessex. By November, Edward had carried the war into East Anglia, where 'all the raiding-army' swore to keep the peace thereafter, and 'the raiding-army that belonged to Cambridge individually' chose Edward as their 'lord and protector, and confirmed that with oaths...'.[87]

It was Aethelflaed's role at this point to contain the Vikings further north – hence the attack on Derby. It was a bitter fight, where 'four of her thegns, who were dear to her, were killed there inside the gates'. But at the end of it, 'God helping', she 'took possession of the stronghold, together with all that belonged to it'.[88] If we discount a raid into Lincolnshire in 909, to carry off the relics of St Oswald, the attack on Derby was the first time that Aethelflaed went on the offensive, and took the war to the enemy.

This first time was also the last. When, in the following year, she led out her army to attack the Danish-held town of Leicester, the Danes surrendered to her without a fight, 'peaceably', and 'the most part of the raiding-armies that belonged to it were subjected'.

(This last comment of the chronicler indicates one reason the Mercians and other Anglo-Saxons experienced such difficulty in containing the Vikings. The Saxons were never dealing with a single unified entity, but with various autonomous armies and warrior bands.[89])

There was more to Aethelflaed's life and work than fending off Vikings. For over seven years, she kept a kingdom running. To understand what this entailed for an early medieval ruler like Aethelflaed, it's useful to look at bishop Asser's list of some of her father's regular activities, while Alfred was king of Wessex. When not on the battlefield, the tireless Alfred found time to meet with his advisers, hold court and hear legal appeals; attend Mass; welcome foreign visitors; hunt, and oversee the work of his huntsmen and falconers; learn Latin and translate books; direct builders, jewel makers and craftsmen; do his accounts; dispense charity, and found a school.

Even if Aethelflaed did not follow her father's punishing schedule, she clearly shared his gifts for systematic organisation and for getting things done. We can be fairly sure she attended to all the tasks of running a kingdom with the same thoroughness she brought to her strategy for building burhs. There were meetings with her council of advisers, her witan, composed of high-ranking laymen and clergy. Laymen who took part in the witan were ealdormen, and those thegns – either landowners or household officers and other high-ranking servants – who belonged to her close circle. Many thegns, but not all, were fighting men. Some were retained as experienced advisers, once their fighting days were over.[90]

She would have held regular meetings with her bishops. Apart from their religious duties, in tenth-century England, churchmen played a number of secular roles. They might be correspondence secretaries to a ruler, or even to the landlord of a large estate. Bishops both witnessed and drafted charters and other legal documents, on behalf of rulers. As the most educated people in a kingdom where few could read English, let alone the Latin necessary for work in government, they interpreted the law and sometimes administered it. (A bishop regularly served on the panel of a shire court, for instance.) For the last few years of his life, Worcester's bishop Waerferth would no doubt have attended Aethelflaed's witan. Another bishop, Aelfwine, who held the diocese of Lichfield during Aethelflaed's years as Lady of the Mercians, and who would later draft charters in the 920s for Aethelflaed's nephew King Athelstan, probably did similar work for Aethelflaed.

Where did the witan meet? As a place associated with centuries of Mercian ancestral tradition, Tamworth was undoubtedly an important royal centre. Aethelflaed was at Tamworth when she died. It was where she would travel to meet with her subjects in the north of her kingdom. Very likely the military campaign against Derby was launched from there. As previously mentioned, the other place of great importance – not least because of Aethelflaed's husband's Hwiccan ancestry – was the royal palace at Kingsholm, just outside the burh walls of newly-refounded Gloucester, half a mile northeast of the town. Continuous use is associated with the site; a witan is known to have met at Gloucester in 896, possibly at Aethelred and Aethelflaed's Kingsholm residence, and the palace was regularly used by later rulers, until the thirteenth century. Edward the Confessor several times convened meetings of his council at Kingsholm. After the Norman conquest of England, William I launched his Domesday survey from there.[91]

What did the witan discuss? Burhs and Vikings, no doubt; and taxes. The granting of licences to trade, and other means of promoting commerce. The appointment of judges and town officials. Relations with neighbouring kingdoms, including Wessex.

Many matters, apart from foreign diplomacy, were settled at local level; but one would imagine that Aethelflaed liked to ensure the affairs of her kingdom ran properly. The main source of a ruler's income was from tolls and taxes. (After a large quantity of Anglo-Saxon coins was found near the Kingsholm palace site in 1784, it was suggested that at one time, Kingsholm might have been a centre for collection of some of these.) She would scarcely fail to keep a close eye on that income, or to distribute gifts to loyal subjects, and funds to religious foundations, much as her father had done in Wessex. She also would make grants to those wishing to engage in trade, as she and Aethelred had done for Bishop Waerferth in 899, giving him land in London on the waterfront enabling him to do business with the Continent.[92]

Anglo-Saxon rulers found it important to reward the loyalty of high-status followers with gifts, which may have taken a variety of forms – from a grant of land, to a decree exempting the recipient from some toll or levy. (Bishop Waerferth, for instance, had once received from King Alfred an exemption, in his Worcester diocese, from the traditional obligation to fund the upkeep of the royal horses and their grooms when in the area.[93])

Generous as it often was, the giving tended to have strings attached. One requirement that generally went with a land grant, for instance, was for the beneficiary to organise and fund (or possibly have his tenants fund) public services – usually meaning the repair of bridges, the building and upkeep of fortifications, or the provision of men to guard the burhs and serve in the *fyrd* (the army). It was an effective way of ensuring the defence of the kingdom was kept up.

Inevitably, much of a ruler's life was lived in public. Even attendance at Mass and other religious observances were activities conducted in the public eye. At the great feasts of Easter, Whitsun and Christmas, Aethelflaed not only presided over meetings of her witan, but also hosted gatherings at one or other of the royal centres, at Gloucester, or at Tamworth, with banqueting and entertainment – for her Mercian kin and other high-status Mercians, and for visitors from farther afield. Generous hospitality was expected of any Saxon ruler. One imagines she would have welcomed guests from neighbouring kingdoms for reasons of diplomacy, and in keeping with the tradition set by the cosmopolitan court of Alfred her father.

A lot of time was spent travelling. The Lady of the Mercians moved around among the towns of her kingdom, inspecting fortifications, and their state of preparedness against attack; ordering construction of new defences or the repair of existing ones; holding court in the various royal centres, and hearing petitions from her subjects. She saw to it that the roads were well maintained between towns. Access to Worcester from Gloucester would have been possible by river, up the Severn. From there it was a day's ride to Warwick, protected by her thegns and accompanied by other members of her household. She could have stayed overnight at Warwick, before riding on to Tamworth. The construction of burhs made such journeys increasingly less hazardous, with strongly fortified places to rest at, and shorter distances between them.

While Aetheflaed's court may not have been the intellectual hub that her father's was, she certainly entertained visitors from Ireland, and from the Welsh kingdoms that paid tribute to her and her brother. There would also have been envoys from neighbouring kingdoms, with whose rulers she was negotiating. Long after her own day, she was remembered by medieval chroniclers for her skills in building military alliances:

> *Aethelflaed, through her own cleverness, made peace with the men of Alba and with the Britons, so that whenever the same race* [the Vikings] *should come to attack her, they would rise to help her. If it were against them that they came, she would take arms with them.*[94]

In about 914, a few years before the end of her life, in a bid to contain Viking raids on Mercia from the north, Aethelflaed had formed alliances with King Constantine of the Scots, with the Cumbric-speaking Christian rulers of the kingdom of Strathclyde, and with the Anglian kingdom of Bernicia, centred on Bamburgh, to the southeast of Strathclyde. The Irish no doubt appreciated her careful watch over the upper reaches of the Mersey and the Dee, keeping open access to the key trading port of Chester. Even Welsh kings, who had suffered cruelly from Saxon oppression in the past, were willing to form at least temporary pacts with her to resist Viking raids.

The Lady of the Mercians also acted as a judge. She was the court of appeal of last resort, for reviewing the judgements of the local Hundreds, and the shire courts.[95] We do not know how often she heard legal appeals, nor whether her rulings were harsh or lenient. One would like to think they were based on principles of fairness – and no one can doubt that she was astute. We have no record of Aethelflaed making, or altering, any contemporary laws. Perhaps she was not an innovator in that sense.

Despite the frequent Viking incursions, under Aethelflaed's rule early tenth-century Mercia had a thriving economy. One indication of this is the number of mints for issuing coins. In Aethelflaed's reign there came to be nine towns in Mercia, not counting Oxford and London, that possessed a mint. Mercia produced coins with distinctive designs not found elsewhere. Though bearing images of King Edward as Aethelflaed's overlord on one side, the reverse shows either a flower or a castle keep; the latter thought by some to be an allusion to the burh-building activities of the Lady of the Mercians. Tellingly, these coins ceased to be produced after Aethelflaed's death.[96]

The kingdom was highly productive. The rich soil of the Midlands was ideal not only for field crops – wheat, barley, flax, beans and oats – but for fruit orchards, and the pasturing of cattle, sheep, and the pigs that fed on acorns in the woods. Fish were abundant in the great rivers that also gave access to trade with Ireland and the western ports of Wessex. Mercia had salt mines, and lead mines producing export-quality lead. Then there were the products of skilled craft workers – potters, smiths and stonemasons, embroiderers and weavers. Fine-quality woollen cloth was another valued Mercian product.

Trade was not all one way. Luxury goods flowed into Mercia from the Continent: ceramics from Belgium, wine from France and Italy, rich silks from Byzantium. All this trade was strictly regulated by law, and subject to taxation. Aethelflaed's kingdom probably followed the laws of Wessex, whereby traders were only permitted to begin trading after making themselves known to the king's reeve at 'a public assembly' – probably the Hundred. Presumably the point was to make sure they paid tax on their transactions. (King Edward's laws further laid down that no one might trade 'except in a market town', where the town reeve or 'other men of credit' might vouch for them – a ruling that may have extended to Mercia.[97]) Along with the various taxes and tolls, fines were prescribed for breaches of the law – all of which made for an increased flow of wealth into Aethelflaed's coffers.

The new burhs made them the safest places to trade and, with their newly laid-out streets and designated market spaces, the most convenient. Given these advantages it should come as no surprise that by the eleventh century, ten per cent of the Mercian population were town dwellers. When new towns became burhs, eventually they gave their names to English shires. By the eleventh century Oxford, Hereford, Chester, Stafford, Warwick and Leicester had become county towns in this way. Thus Aethelflaed, as well as founding and refounding their urban centres, may be said to have created counties in the Midlands.[98]

The towns flourished across her kingdom, kept safe within her burh walls, and later spread out beyond them. Stafford had its own mint by the mid-900s, greatly enhancing the town's prosperity and that of the surrounding area. In 1206 it would be granted a royal charter. Gloucester owes to Aethelflaed the very existence of its market centre, with its four intersecting main streets named for the city gates, and the grid of smaller streets around them. Tamworth, the royal capital of the Mercians in the north, would become a bustling market town, that honours her contribution to its founding by a statue, and holds occasional celebrations in her memory.[99]

If she could see what has grown from her efforts to defend her kingdom and enable it to prosper – the flourishing centres that, thanks to her work as a founder still exist today, the Lady of the Mercians could justly be proud.

CHAPTER FIVE

Lady of the Church

'To those who uphold this shall be added the reward of eternal bliss in heaven.'[100]

In the dimly lit wooden building thick with incense, Aethelflaed kneels on the flagstones between her mother and younger sisters. Behind them, the ranks of noblemen, thegns and peasants kneel too. One by one, the adults get to their feet and file up to take Communion – the royal members of Aethelflaed's family first, followed by the nobles and thegns, the household servants, then the rest.

It's the fifth Sunday in Lent. In memory of Christ's fast in the wilderness, Aethelflaed and her family have been living on a diet of beans and lentils, with a little fish every Friday. At this time of year, believers are urged to cleanse themselves by 'fasts, and holy vigils', by meditating on the scriptures and giving to charity, 'that there may not be found in us any place devoid of spiritual power, wherein wicked vices may dwell'. In the monasteries, they're preaching against worldly desire and excessive love of the world – not without stern warnings of eternal damnation for those who disobey God's commands.[101]

Even by West Saxon standards, Aethelflaed's family are unusually pious. Her father has translated classic Christian texts from Latin into English for the benefit of lay people all over his kingdom. He has endowed schools, so that boys may learn to read the scriptures in Latin. Aethelflaed's mother, too, is known for her generosity and her piety. Aethelflaed's sister Aethelgifu will become an abbess, in the convent their father has founded at Shaftesbury. That might have been

67

Aethelflaed's path in life too, if matters had turned out differently. As it is, the king has seen to it that all his daughters, equally with his sons, are literate in religious matters. Aethelflaed, now in her teens, can read familiar religious texts in Latin. She can recite the Lord's Prayer, knows many psalms by heart, and whole chunks of the Gospels. Along with the Latin phrases of the Mass, these words are woven into the fabric of her everyday world.[102]

In all the Anglo-Saxon kingdoms, before the Viking raids, the church was wealthy, its richly endowed churches and religious houses benefiting from the patronage of royal families. It remains politically powerful in the Anglo-Saxon world, owing to the support it draws from the Pope and his entourage in Rome; but that support also makes it subject to Rome's jurisdiction. Directives come regularly from there to far-off England – about washing after sexual intercourse and before attending Mass; about which distant relatives may marry one another without committing a sin; about burial of the dead. More injunctions and interpretations of Christian teaching come from nearer home, from manuals and homilies composed by the native clergy.[103]

Besides the communications from Rome that affect all believers, the royal family of Wessex have their own more personal connections with the Roman hierarchy. Aethelflaed's father was taken there as a child of only 4 years old, and blessed by Pope Leo. Two years later, he went again. He will surely have told Aethelflaed and his other children as much as he can remember about these adventures. In adult life Alfred has sent financial contributions, 'alms', to Pope Marinus who, 'as a result of the friendship and entreaties' of the Saxon king, has exempted Rome's English residents from taxation. As a further token of goodwill, the pope has sent Alfred a fragment of the True Cross on which Christ was crucified.[104]

Wessex also takes religious cultural cues from the powerful kingdom of the Franks. Alfred's family intermarry with them, and respectfully imitate their customs. Young nobles from the Frankish kingdom are sent to gain an education at Alfred's court. Here, they benefit from the presence of scholars like Bishop Asser from Wales, and the highly educated Grimbald, a priest and monk from Gaul, 'extremely learned in every kind of ecclesiastical doctrine and in the Holy Scriptures'. King Alfred corresponds with Fulco, archbishop of Rheims, and with Elias, Patriarch of Jerusalem. It all makes for a cosmopolitan environment, connecting Aethelflaed and her family to the wider world of Christendom. Religious life at the court of Aethelflaed's father may be carried on a long way from the centre, but its atmosphere is far from provincial.[105]

Some of the pious visitors are quite eccentric. In 891, Alfred received three pilgrims from Ireland, who had drifted ashore in Cornwall, 'in a boat without oars', and headed for the Wessex court. They had left Ireland, they said, because they wanted 'for the love of God to be abroad' – they did not care where. On arriving in Cornwall, they had set out to find King Alfred, who made them welcome for a while. Then they had left again, saying they hoped to make it to Rome. Such holy wanderers, known as 'pilgrims for the love of God', are actually not that uncommon. If Aethelflaed did not meet this particular group – by 891 she is married and living in Mercia – she might, in her younger days, have encountered others like them.[106]

Every day of Aethelflaed's home life is filled with religious observance. Her family pray together morning and evening. Time is set aside, too, for private meditation. Aethelflaed may well take to heart the priest's advice to bless herself with the sign of the cross at intervals during the day. Does she know that her father often slips out secretly at night, to pray alone in some empty church? If she has heard of this habit of his, it surely will not surprise her. His piety is legendary.

Alfred is also famously prone to religious guilt. When in his youth, before marriage, Alfred realised he was at the mercy of his sexual desires and 'unable to abstain', he was filled with a sense of his own sinfulness. He became deeply afraid of God's anger. Often, he would go out at dawn to prostrate himself on the floor of some church, 'praying that Almighty God through his mercy would more staunchly strengthen his resolve in the love of His service by means of some illness'. The agonising pain that first struck Alfred on the day of his wedding, and disabled him at intervals until his mid-forties, may possibly have been psychosomatic in origin, the body's response to an anxious prayer.[107]

They may be less guilt-ridden than Alfred, but everyone around Aethelflaed constantly prays for help in every human activity. Prayers are said for the sick or the dying, for guidance in difficult decisions, for a blessing on a newborn child, for protection against demons. And against Vikings, who in many people's estimation are probably much the same thing, and a good deal nearer home. In 875, Bishop Waerferth of Worcester organised prayers for the sins of Mercia's Viking-sponsored puppet ruler, Ceolwulf II, and called on God for Anglo-Saxon lands to be saved from the heathen invaders.[108]

There are always prayers before battle. Alfred's older brother, King Aethelred, famously nearly missed the fight with the Vikings at Ashdown in 871, because he was praying – 'declaring firmly that he would not leave that place alive before the priest had finished Mass, and that he would not forsake divine service for that of men'.[109]

Prayer is more than a merely personal matter. Regular prayer and even personal spirituality, along with practice of the Christian virtues, are an aspect of the defence of the realm, every bit as much as forts and armies. A kingdom, in the view of Aethelflaed's father, needs devout men and women, as much as farmers and soldiers.[110] In 886, Bishop Waerferth arranged for daily prayers to be said for Mercia's new ruler, Aethelflaed's husband Lord Aethelred.

Women have their own books for private devotions. Two are still in existence today, that appear to have been intended for women – and possibly written by them. One of these may have belonged to Aethelflaed's mother Ealhswith. The so-called Book of Nunnaminster, named after the abbey that Ealhswith founded, is linked to Ealhswith by a sketch plan in it, of land in Winchester owned by her, and corresponding to the area where the Nunnaminster was built. The book contains a few Latin words in their feminine forms, included as if by accident, where the standard usage would be masculine. (Possibly the female scribe unconsciously slipped into writing as a woman?[111])

The Nunnaminster Book begins with passages from the Gospels, followed by appeals to the saints, and meditations on the life, death and resurrection of Jesus, on Pentecost and on the Last Judgement. Several verses or hymns come next, followed by a group of prayers asking God to inform and guide various parts of the body. More unusually, there is then a prayer for protection from the poison of reptiles and 'venomous flies'.

The overall tone of the Nunnaminster Book is on the gloomy side. One prayer to the Virgin Mary, for instance, asks for the worshipper to be enabled to avoid 'the dark shadows of hell' ('inferni tenebras evadere'). Another prays that the believer's ears may never have to hear the terrible words, 'Depart from me ye cursed into everlasting fire.' There is, it is true, an affirmation of faith in God's protection for the devout Christian, in a prayer containing the words, 'No one can prevail against me'; and one of thanksgiving, in a prayer to be said at Pentecost. But most of the texts carry a heavy undertone of anxiety about sin, and of unworthiness before God.[112] Are these writings perhaps designed to aid the meditations of a woman facing the end of her life, to whom the prospect of judgement after death looms large? We know that shortly after founding her Nunnaminster, Ealhswith died.

Not all surviving Anglo-Saxon prayer books are as dark in tone as the Nunnaminster Book. Others express joy. The 'Royal Manuscript', for example, contains a litany of praise to Christ, 'who after death leads us into everlasting rejoicing ('ducit nos post obitum In gaudium sempiternum'). Prayers in the 'Harley Manuscript' sound a similar hopeful note. A short hymn or poem in this manuscript, simply titled 'Oratio', is a comforting prayer for the night: 'May I sleep in the peace of Christ, and see no evil or harmful night visions, but a vision divine and prophetic':

> In pace Christi dormiam
> ut nullum malum videam
> a malis visionibus
> in noctibus nocentibus,
> Sed visionem videam
> divinam ac propheticam.[113]

71

Aethelflaed will be familiar with many similar prayers invoking protection before sleep. She also probably knows about healing through the recitation of set formulae. Some of these have an incantatory quality, more like magical charms or spells. A prayer to stop bleeding, for instance, with its rhythmic repetition of the words 'flumen' and 'flumina' (river/rivers):

> *flumina flumen aridum veruens flumen pallidum parens*
> *flumen rubrum acriter de corpore exiens restringe tria*
> *flumina flumen cruorem restrigantem nervos limentem cicatricis*
> *concupiscente timores fugante per dominum*
> *nostrum Ihesum Christum.* [114]

If Aethelflaed has absorbed any of the religious anxieties of her parents, nothing in what we know of her life seems to indicate this. And regardless of the attitudes to faith of either of her parents, the wider religious culture that surrounds her contains as much of hope and gladness as it does of preoccupation with punishment and sin. Christmas, Easter and Pentecost are all times of celebration. On these festival occasions Aethelflaed's father holds court at one of his royal 'vills', or residences – Chippenham, perhaps, or Winchester. For a few days, all work in the fields comes to a standstill. At court there is feasting, with gatherings of family and guests at Alfred's generous table. There is chanting and singing in the churches, and more secular music, with songs and recitations in the great hall. While, even for those of high status, life in ninth-century Wessex can be harsh and tragic, it can also contain moments of joy.

One great source of comfort and inspiration for the Anglo-Saxon people as they face a grave military threat, is the 'Old Testament', the Hebrew Bible. In the challenges that will confront her in later life, Aethelflaed may, like her father, turn for strength to the Old Testament prophets and the psalms of David, many of which have been translated by Alfred himself, from a Latin version of the Bible. 'I shall rejoice and exult, and extol Your name, Almighty God! / For you threw back my enemies; and they were weakened, and perished before your face'; 'The Lord is our protection and our strength and our support in our tribulations ... / Therefore we shall not fear, even though all the earth is oppressed and the mountains are cast into the middle of the sea.' Words like these might well give Alfred's daughter courage before battle, as they inspired her father.[115]

A cult of the saints is central to the faith of the Anglo-Saxons. In these harsh and threatening times, those most venerated are men and women who in their lifetimes distinguished themselves by their courage. Not only devout women, like Juliana or St Barbara, who died rather than renounce Christianity, but military men like Oswald, defeated by a pagan and cut down in battle; or martyred apostles like St Andrew, who remained steadfast even when his trust in God was challenged.[116] These tales of heroic endurance draw not only upon Christian ideals, but upon a deep-rooted pre-Christian warrior tradition. In this tradition, the courageous man who goes down fighting becomes a legend, remembered and celebrated by his people long after his death.

Accepting death non-violently for the Christian faith was not conceived of as mere passive victimhood, either. The ultimate model for the ideal of martyrdom is that of Christ himself. A well-known eighth-century poem, 'The Dream of the Rood' – a poem that Aethelflaed may have known – fuses Christian and pre-Christian traditions in its image of Christ as a young warrior hero confronting his final battle. The 'Rood', the cross on which Jesus is to die, is the narrator in the poem. It bears witness to Christ's heroic courage:

> The young man, Heaven's King, cast off his clothes,
> strong and firm spirited; he stood on the gallows
> bravely, beheld by many, to break mankind free.

As judge of souls in the next world, the risen Christ will challenge those who stand before him there. Have they shown themselves capable of following his example?

None may be boldly unafraid
of the words the Lord will speak:
he will ask the many there if each man
dare, for his name, know death's
bitter taste as he did on the tree.
They will be afraid then, and have few thoughts
of what they could say to Christ.

There is no need for fear, however, the Rood reassures the listeners. Anyone who has faith in the saving power of the Cross will be received by Christ:

None there need fear
if they bear in their breast the holy beacon;
through that cross heaven's kingdom
each soul will seek from earth
that is willing to worship the Lord.[117]

As shown by the death of King Alfred's contemporary King Edmund, the question of martyrdom for Anglo-Saxons is more than a theoretical one. Whether, as in his legend, Edmund really died at the hands of the Viking invaders because he refused to renounce his Christian faith, or simply because the Danes wanted his lands, his contemporaries considered him a holy martyr; he was soon canonised as a saint.

No doubt Aethelflaed reveres and honours the holy martyrs – though one tends to think that if she were facing an unpleasant death and given the choice between martyrdom and taking a few Vikings with her, she might, being the kind of person she was, prefer to have the chance of putting up a fight.

Religious faith, in Aethelflaed's world, was expressed not only in the litanies and legends of the church, but in popular culture – in proverbial wisdom. The Exeter Book, a tenth-century collection of poems, riddles and proverbial sayings, contains maxims or 'gnomes', many of which surely pre-date the time of its compilation. One of these maxims expresses a devout trust in the just order of things:

Left: 'Aethelflaed', by Anna Fenn, from the E2BN 'History's Heroes' website. (historysheroes.e2bn.orgherowhowerethey4292)

Right: Æthelflæd, Cartulary of Abingdon Abbey, thirteenth century. (British Library MS, Cotton Claudius B VI folio 14r)

Detail from Aethelflaed window in St Andrew's, Churchdown. George Cooper-Abbs, 1934.

Aethelflaed of Mercia, AD 917. (Gambargin, Women War Queens series)

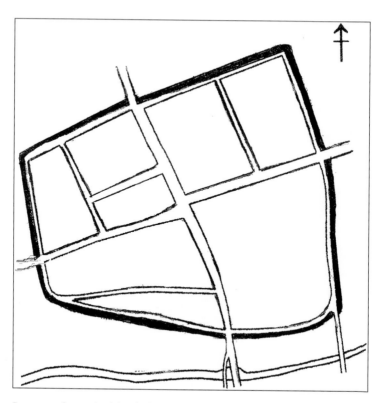

Layout of a typical burh, based on the burh at Oxford.

The Market Cross, Gloucester, with St Michael's Tower.

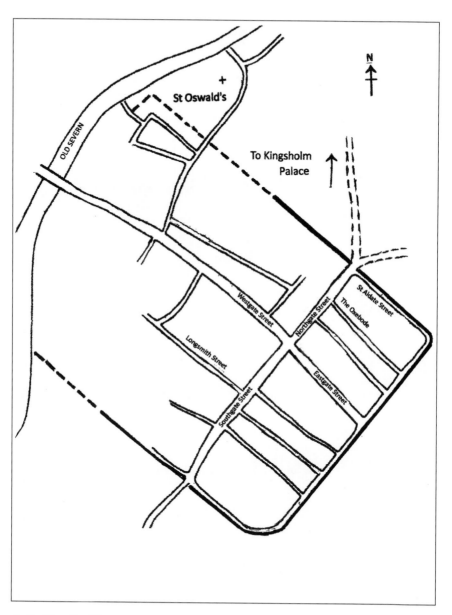

Aethelflaed's Gloucester.

Plaque in Castle Street, Warwick, commemorating Aethelflaed's founding of the town in 914.

City wall, Chester.

Aethelflaed's burhs and battles, 900s to 917.

Detail from Steve Field's Caryatid Gate, Wednesbury.

Æthelflæd in a thirteenth-century genealogy. (British Library, MS Royal14 B V)

'La Sage'
Aethelflaed, in a
fourteenth-century
genealogy.
(British Library,
MS Royal 14 B VI)

St Oswald's Priory, Gloucester.

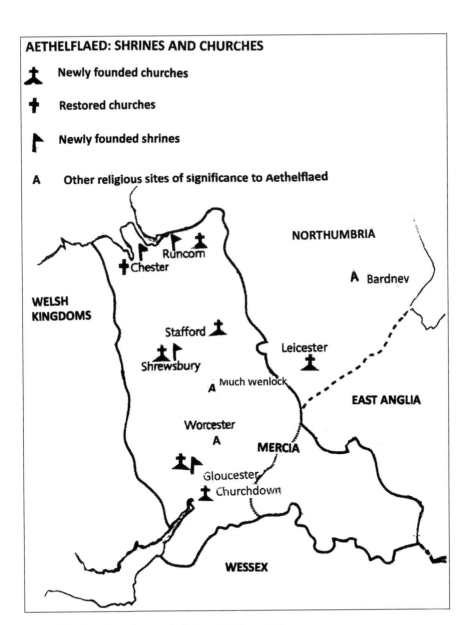

Aethelflaed – Churches and shrines, 900s to 918.

'Ethelfleda' in Chester cathedral by
W.T. Carter Shapland.

Aethelflaed statue by Edward George Bramwell (1913), in Tamworth.

Earl Ferrers unveiling the Tamworth statue in 1913. Reproduced in Tamworth Herald, 18 January 2013.

Millenary pageant procession in Tamworth 1913. Tamworth Herald, January 2013.

Ethelfleda Bridge, Runcorn.

Holding back the Vikings at Runcorn.

Aethelflaed taking hostages at Brecon Mere (Llangorse) By Richard Caton Woodville, in Hutchinson's Story of the British Nation, 1922.

Ethelfleda Terrace, Wednesbury.

Left: 'Ethelfloeda'. Detail of Benjamin Fletcher's sculpture of 1922, in Leicester.

Right: Watch on the Mersey. Angela Sidwell's sculpture at Runcorn.

Wrought iron fence on Runcorn waterfront.

Aethelflaed Gruit Ale. Advertisement designed by Jose Carmona. (Courtesy of Sacre Brew Co.)

Aethelflaed models for Bad Squiddo games.

> *To us God is everlasting,*
> *Fates change him not. Nothing affects him,*
> *neither age nor illness, the Almighty,*
> *nor does he grow old in spirit, but he is still as he was,*
> *a patient prince.*[118]

Another set of maxims alludes to the diversity of human societies under God:

> *He gives us thoughts,*
> *different dispositions, several tongues;*
> *an isle holds many in its wide embrace,*
> *various races of people. These broad lands*
> *the Lord set forth for humankind,*
> *the Almighty God, as manifold of both kindred and customs.*[119]

Does Aethelflaed perhaps think of some saying like this when she mingles with foreign visitors at her father's court; or later on in her life, when negotiating an alliance with some neighbouring kingdom?

One saying praises peace-makers: 'They ever settle strife, they that preach peace / which wicked men have previously wrecked.'[120] Is there an allusion to the Vikings here – 'wicked men', who bring strife and suffering? The Danes and Norsemen were not demonised because they were racially 'other'. They were resisted because they plundered and killed. (They were, admittedly, regarded as *religiously* other, however, and their ruthless behaviour was regularly attributed to the fact that they were not Christians.) But their true offence was to shatter the peace, committing acts of violence and cruelty, in quest of material gain.[121]

Religion entered into the legal, as well as the moral, sphere. Every important act performed according to law in the Anglo-Saxon world, whether testifying on oath in a court, or signing a contract, was accompanied by an invocation of God as a witness. Such invocations were written into the text of official documents. When Waerferth, bishop of Worcester, in 904 grants land in Worcester to Aethelflaed and her husband Aethelred, the charter specifying the terms of the grant ends with both a promise and a warning. To those who honour the agreement is offered 'the reward of eternal bliss in heaven'. Anyone violating its terms, however, will be 'confounded by eternal punishment', unless 'they have made due amends'. Those signing the document have then witnessed its blessing 'with the symbol of the cross of Christ'.[122]

One element in Anglo-Saxon religion that may seem puzzling, even troubling, to modern sensibilities is the apparent ease with which it mingled materialism with its undoubted piety. Monasteries and convents were founded by, and remained the prerogative of, royal and aristocratic families who received income from the profits of abbey lands. The appointment of abbots and abbesses was equally in the gift of their royal founders. The ease, moreover, with which Anglo-Saxon royal families canonised their family members as saints – a sort of spiritual nepotism, at a time when canonisation was purely a local matter, rather than something determined in Rome – may seem troubling.

Not only was a portion of the revenues accruing to religious establishments claimed by the founders as a right, but bishops like Waerferth of Worcester, or the bishop of London, personally owned large tracts of land. Sometimes they got into inheritance or land boundary disputes with other clergy.[123] High-ranking clergy also regularly engaged in trade with continental Europe. They might, like Waerferth in his dealings with Aethelred and Aethelflaed as Lord and Lady of the Mercians, petition the ruler for exemptions from tolls and taxes. Archbishops even had the right to issue currency, the coins they minted being stamped with their names.

Such practices may well appear to us contradictory, even corrupt, in their determination to serve both God and Mammon to the limit, and to have travelled some way from the ideals and practices of Christianity's founder. This is not to say that the Anglo-Saxons were insincere or cynical in their beliefs, or that high-status individuals did not in other respects try to live Christian lives.

Alms-giving and other forms of generosity were central to the Anglo-Saxon way of life. 'Loathed is he who lays claim to land, dear is he who donates more', runs one maxim preserved in the Exeter Book.[124] It was also good to 'give gold':

> *One ought to give gold away. God can grant*
> *possessions to the prosperous and take them back again.*[125]

The tradition of generosity built upon an earlier pre-Christian tradition of *noblesse oblige*, in which a 'ring-giver', a king or leader who gave generously to honour and show appreciation of his followers, was worthy of the highest praise. For an Anglo-Saxon ruler in the ninth and tenth centuries, the earlier pagan imperative to be generous was reinforced by Christian teaching on charity. 'God loves a cheerful giver', Asser quotes from Corinthians in his *Life* of King Alfred.[126]

Aethelflaed's father was a model 'giver'. With the methodical approach that marked all his doings, Alfred sat down one day and arranged systematically to divide up his annual income. Half of it was allotted for payment of soldiers and thegns, for craftsmen, and for foreign visitors in need. The other half, he reserved for alms to the poor, for the school he had founded, for upkeep of the monastery at Athelney and the convent at Shaftesbury, and for other monasteries in England and as far afield as Ireland and Gaul.

Aethelflaed followed her father's example, by building and endowing shrines and churches. Concrete evidence of the first, and most famous, of these endowments – a project shared with her husband Aethelred, can still be seen in Gloucester. In the early 900s Aethelred and Aethelflaed founded the priory of St Peter's, soon to be renamed St Oswald's, which became popularly known as 'the New Minster', and later 'the Golden Minster', for the splendour of its decorations and the wealth it brought to Gloucester and the church. This endowment would be only the first of many.[127]

It is unclear, from the terse account in the *Anglo-Saxon Chronicles*, whether Aethelflaed played any part in the daring raid of 909 into Viking territory at Bardney in Lincolnshire, when the relics of St Oswald preserved there were carried back in triumph to Gloucester and installed in St Peter's/St Oswald's. All we are told in the *Anglo-Saxon Chronicles* is that Oswald's body 'was brought from Bardney into Mercia'. (The exact circumstances in which the relics were obtained are equally unclear – whether they were carried off after a fight, or handed over by a pious custodian, or even purchased from some non-religious vendor, into whose hands they might have fallen.) It's possible that Aethelflaed at least led Mercian forces into the Danelaw. She may have participated in an actual raid.

Bardney had been a Mercian monastery, and the Mercians would have had a special interest in recovering the saint's remains. Aethelflaed would certainly have had a major voice in the installation of the relics in the newly built minster, its name changed from St Peter's to St Oswald's in the saint's honour.

However it came about, St Oswald's bones duly arrived in Gloucester. Or some of them did. When this seventh-century warrior king and saint was killed in single combat with the pagan Mercian king Penda, his head and arms were severed from his body and displayed by the victor as trophies. (The head ended up at the monastery in Lindisfarne in Northumbria, and one of the arms at the former site of Oswald's court in Northumbrian Bamburgh.) Even a headless torso, however, was a powerful religious talisman. Its return to Mercia would have been considered a triumph.

To the modern sensibility, the preservation and display of body parts of the dead in places of worship may seem strange – ghoulish even. The practice undoubtedly led to all kinds of fraud, and had by the time of the Reformation in the sixteenth century become thoroughly corrupt, with various religious institutions laying claim to multiple versions of some saint's head or right arm, for the wealth it brought them. But early medieval societies believed that a person who had benefited others in this life could confer even greater blessing from the next world when they were presumably closer to God. Preserving their body parts, or sometimes parts of their possessions, was a way to try and maintain a connection between the deceased saint and a worshipping community.

Around the founding of the New Minster, and its dedication to St Oswald, scholarly arguments have swirled. Why did Aethelflaed and Aethelred choose to build in Gloucester? Why install the relics of this particular saint? There have been ingenious theories. Perhaps the Mercian rulers avoided building at the more important Mercian royal centre of Tamworth for fear of antagonising Aethelflaed's brother King Edward who, after Alfred died, had become their overlord? Establishing an important new minster at Tamworth, according to this theory, could have been read as a Mercian claim to independence from the kingdom of Wessex. There still was a degree of assertion of such independence in creating the mausoleum at the Gloucester church, where Aethelflaed and her husband wished to be buried at their deaths. Aethelflaed had still made a somewhat defiant decision – her body would not lie in a grave back in the Wessex family mausoleum at Winchester, but beside that of her husband in his Gloucestershire homeland.[128]

Another theory about the choice to site Oswald's remains in Gloucester argues for water symbolism. Oswald was killed by the banks of a tributary of the River Severn, the great river that flows through Gloucester city. So, the argument goes, in view of legendary associations between Oswald, his relics, and sacred streams, the saint's presence in Gloucester symbolically brought a blessing to 'flow' there.[129]

The reasons, both for building at Gloucester and for the 'translation' of Oswald's relics there, seem a lot more straightforward. As a leading member of the Mercian tribe of the Hwicce, Aethelred was more at home in Gloucestershire, where his ancestors were buried, than in the traditional centre of Mercian power in the north, at Tamworth. His royal residence, with its central meeting hall, was established in Gloucester within walking distance of the New Minster. What could be more natural, therefore, than to build a shrine at the minster and to install the bones there – and hopefully to bring with them the blessings of the famous saint?

Oswald's own generous charity was part of his legend. When a crowd of hungry people once gathered outside his palace, it is said that he ordered the food from his table to be taken out to them, and the silverware from the meal to be broken up and distributed too. His mentor, the saintly Aidan, was with him at the time and supposedly exclaimed, pointing to Oswald, 'May this hand never wither with age.' Or so the story goes. After his death, Oswald's body was said to have remained uncorrupted for many years after burial – a common early medieval tradition associated with sainthood.[130]

Was Oswald's legendary generosity perhaps part of his appeal for Aethelflaed? The saint was also said to work miracles from beyond the grave, nearly all associated with healing. Stories were told of how sick people were cured by drinking water mixed with dust from the site where St Oswald had been killed in battle. He was said to have ended a plague in a stricken community who prayed for help from the saint.

It wasn't all about piety, charity and healing, however. A saint could have political influence, even after death. Oswald was popular in Mercia – not least in the formerly Mercian territories long since absorbed into the Danelaw. He was, moreover, the son of a Northumbrian king and it was believed, correctly or otherwise, that Aethelflaed was herself descended from the Northumbrian royal house through her father's maternal ancestors.[131]

Now his remains were safe in Gloucester, liberated from the clutches of 'the heathen' in Lincolnshire, Oswald's legend could be a rallying point for the Mercian and Northumbrian peoples to unite and defend themselves against the Danes. It is surely no accident that the new church was built within easy riding or walking distance from the royal palace at Kingsholm, with a straight track running for half a mile between the two sites.

Just a year after the saint's relics arrived in Gloucester, a Mercian army defeated Danish raiders on 5 August, St Oswald's feast day. The Mercian people could hardly have failed to find meaning in this coincidence. The saint was, it seemed, already doing his job of protecting them from harm.

Little remains of St Oswald's Priory today – only a few of the original stones in part of a single freestanding wall. With the help of a display board thoughtfully provided by Gloucester City Council, and a little imagination, however, the layout of the original church can still be pictured – its noble line of rounded arches making a shaded gloom of the interior, except where the sun would have streamed in broad bands of light across the stone floor, and with the wide expanse of the River Severn flowing near the western door outside. The minster was not much bigger than the average parish church – 120ft in length, with a ceiling 32ft high. Following the model of the royal mausoleum at the former Mercian capital of Repton in Derbyshire, a separate, square-shaped two-level crypt was built at the east end of the building, to house either the relics of St Oswald or, at some future date, the coffins of the minster's founders.

The church interior was famed for its splendour. Embroidered wall hangings, wall paintings and brightly coloured carvings, the gleam of gold and silver from the precious objects on the altar, incense and candlelight, with the echo of harmonious chanting resounding under the high roof, would have made worshipping in the church an unforgettable experience.

The elaborate painting and gilding, the gleaming candlesticks, the saints' icons, disappeared long ago. Even the tombs and the royal crypt have been 'robbed out' over the centuries. A few beautifully carved stone grave covers and other pieces of stone carving are now in Gloucester city museum. These, and the ruined wall, are all that has survived from Aethelflaed's time. Not only the minster's plundered treasures, but the relics of St Oswald, like nearly all such superstitious objects, vanished from Gloucester at the time of the Reformation. But in its own day, the 'Golden Minster' and its shrine drew pilgrims from far and wide.

A former Mayor of Gloucester is not exaggerating when he describes Aethelflaed's founding of St Oswald's as 'an incredible step forward in the development of the city' – a development that was carried on in later ages, when Gloucester Cathedral in its turn became the new magnet for pilgrims.[132] The visitors came to seek absolution for their sins, a cure for sickness, a blessing, or simply a new experience away from home. For some, the pilgrimage to Gloucester and St Oswald would have been an exotic trip, like going to Thailand or Egypt today. For others, it could have been a profound and transforming spiritual experience. In either case, it clearly was something a lot of people wanted to do – and it generated wealth for Gloucester. Pilgrims made donations to the minster, paid in the town for food and lodging, and no doubt boosted sales of tacky tourist souvenirs – brooches, medallions, rosaries and phials of holy water. After 1066 St Oswald's became a residence and place of worship for a group of devout men known as 'secular canons', who took religious vows to live together under one roof and to pray and work together.

Although the neighbouring abbey church of St Peter, later to become Gloucester's Norman cathedral, gradually upstaged the old Saxon minster, which was falling into ruin by 1541 and demolished a hundred years later, we should remember that in earlier times St Oswald's Minster – later St Oswald's Priory – was a wonder of its age.[133]

Given Aethelred's attachment to Gloucester, and Aethelflaed's contributions to rebuilding and beautifying the town, the local tradition seems credible that Aethelflaed also founded a church in the village of Churchdown a few miles away.[134]

Gloucestershire was far from being the only place where Aethelflaed gave to the church. Every burh she built had its small chapel beside one of the four main gates. If she did not directly fund these places, she certainly promoted their construction. When in 917 and 918 she reclaimed Derby and Leicester from Danish control, she had the churches that had been destroyed by the Vikings rebuilt. In Leicester she is thought to have built or restored on the site of the church that today is called St Mary de Castro. In Tamworth, too, she rebuilt what had been left by Danish invaders as a blackened ruin. One day, long after her death, this Tamworth church would bear the name of Aethelflaed's niece, as St Editha's.[135]

In 901 Aethelflaed and Aethelred granted land, with a valuable chalice, to the nunnery of St Mildburh at Wenlock in Shropshire, in return for prayers to be said for them by the religious community there. We have to wonder what induced Aethelflaed and Aethelred to endow this particular religious house, with its cult of St Mildburh the healer, and her miraculous holy well. Unlike Gloucester, or other towns where Mercian rulers endowed churches and established shrines, Wenlock had no administrative, commercial or military importance. Was Aethelred beginning to be ill by this time? He died ten years later, and Aethelflaed seems gradually to have assumed responsibility for the day-to-day running of the kingdom of Mercia. Perhaps the prayers said for Aethelred at Wenlock were for the healing of his body, as well as his soul?[136]

When Aethelflaed ordered the construction of a burh at Runcorn on the River Mersey, she is said to have brought the supposed remains of the legendary hermit St Beorhthelm to the town. Beorhthelm, or Bertelin, may or may not have actually existed; possibly the bones that came to Runcorn were someone else's? He was believed to have been a prince who had chosen to become a hermit, and gone to live on an island in a bend of the River Sow, in Staffordshire. The legend of his presence on the island is said to have inspired Aethelflaed to found the burh at Stafford. Beorhthelm was equally venerated at Runcorn during the latter part of Aethelflaed's rule as Lady of the Mercians, and she dedicated a new church to him there. A nineteenth-century church, now re-dedicated as the church of All Saints, stands on the site of Aethelflaed's original building. Stafford, too, had a St Bertelin's church at the heart of its new burh – close to where the Collegiate Church of St Mary now stands, near the town centre. (When exactly St Bertelin's was founded is unknown, though it is quite likely that this was the original burh church.[137])

In 907, Chester was refortified, restoring the old Roman walls and building around them. With its own mint, it was an important commercial and administrative centre in northern Mercia, second only to Tamworth. A shrine to St Werburgh was established in the church of St Peter and St Paul in Chester, to house the remains of the saint, brought to the town by the monks of Hanbury in the Repton area. Vikings had raided and settled in Repton, ancestral last resting place of Mercian royalty, in the winter of 873-4 and taken long-term possession of Derby, only nine miles away. As with the removal of Oswald's relics to Gloucester, 'translating' St Werburgh's remains to Chester was a rescue operation, bringing a precious object to safety from the Danelaw.

The church in Chester was later renamed St Werburgh's. (In 1541 it became Chester Cathedral.) The relics were now sited at the very heart of a fortified, protected town, where there was also a shrine to St Oswald. The church became a magnet for pilgrims and Werburgh became Chester's patron saint. To this day, the Cathedral has a St Werburgh shrine, built in the 1800s.

St Werburgh, a much-loved saint with a reputation as a healer, evidently had shared with her devotee Aethelflaed a gift for administration and a commitment to whatever she undertook. She was known as a reformer of Mercian convents. On receiving a premonition of her approaching death, she visited each of the nunneries under her jurisdiction to make sure that everything was in order before she left the world.

St Werburgh's personal qualities, though, were probably less relevant for the Lady of the Mercians than the ancestry she may have shared with the saint. Werburgh's paternal grandfather was the formidable Mercian king Penda, and Aethelflaed may have believed that she too was descended from this powerful Mercian ancestor, through Ealhswith her Mercian mother. Bringing St Werburgh's remains to Chester was a very public way of reclaiming that connection.

Besides Oswald and Werburgh, Aethelflaed probably oversaw, or at least approved, 'translation' of the remains of another putative royal ancestor – St Alkmund. Known by the Anglo-Saxons as Ealhmund, he was a prince of the royal house of Northumbria. He had been buried at Northworthy, the adjoining territory to Derby, an area that continued to be a centre of Saxon community life after the Danes had founded their settlement of Derby. Why Shrewsbury was chosen as the place to move Ealhmund's relics to is unclear. As Northworthy was now part of the Danelaw, however, transferring them out of there to the Welsh border country on the other side of Mercia would have made sense. The church that housed them is still called St Alkmund's today. It stands at the highest point on Shrewsury's burh hill, with a commanding view of the Severn valley. Almost certainly, St Alkmund's did double duty as a spiritual protector and as a military lookout point. It was not until the 1100s that Ealhmund's remains were returned to Derby, and reburied close to their original resting place.

The motives for Aethelflaed's endowment of religious centres with rich gifts and with holy relics, were more than simply a matter of personal piety and individual charity, although no doubt these played their part. It was also a matter of publicly demonstrating her generosity and her power. Important in this regard, was the prestige conferred by the shrines of saints with real or imagined links to revered ancestors. It is no accident that all the saints whose relics Aethelflaed translated – Oswald, Werburgh, Beorhthelm, Ealhmund – were, or were considered to be, of royal descent. If it was thought that Aethelflaed was related to them through her Mercian maternal heritage, it can only have helped her popularity with the Mercian people.

The dedication of St Editha's in Tamworth looks to the generation after Aethelflaed. Editha's brother Athelstan had married her to the Danish king Sihtric of Northumbria, but Sihtric is said to have abandoned both his bride and his new faith of Christianity. Editha then founded a religious community in Tamworth, where she became known for caring for the sick, and other works of charity.

It is unknown what the original burh church in Tamworth was called, only that it was founded by Aethelflaed and built on the site of one burned down by a Viking raid in 874. It seems to have been a favourite target for Vikings, who – burh or no burh – in 943 managed to burn it down again. (By 963, King Edgar had had it rebuilt once more.) Other 'Aethelflaedan' churches are in Bridgnorth, where St Leonard's, though a largely nineteenth-century building, is said to have Saxon stone incorporated in its walls; and St Mary de Castro in Leicester – though it would hardly have been called that when Aethelflaed either founded or rebuilt it.

Shrines and relics were very important in the life of any early tenth-century Anglo-Saxon community. Given people's faith in the power of protection afforded by the presence of a saint, they were, along with the bulwark of prayer, the reassuring spiritual counterpart of forts and burhs. With the buildings that housed them, they had a cultural function too, becoming centres of art and learning. In this regard, they were not so different from King Alfred's project to restore learning to Wessex after the Viking raids.

The new religious foundations were welcome in the towns because of the prosperity they brought, employing masons and other craftsmen and, as at Gloucester, attracting pilgrims and tourism. If the endowments enhanced the reputation of Aethelflaed Lady of the Mercians, they also contributed to the stability of the kingdom of Mercia, sorely needed after years of political turmoil, destruction and war.

We can't understand Aethelflaed without understanding the religious aspects of her world; the centrality to it – with all its blending of piety and materialism, of power politics and sincere devotion – of Christian faith, and the church in which she had been raised. These were integral to everything she did.

CHAPTER SIX

Alfred's Daughter

'Daughters whose fathers have been actively engaged throughout childhood in promoting their achievements and encouraging their self-reliance and assertiveness are more likely to succeed in leadership roles traditionally held by males.'[138]

'I could not as my father's daughter remain indifferent to all that was going on.'[139]

What was it like for Aethelflaed to grow up as the eldest child of a man of tireless energy and enthusiastic scholarship, who defeated Vikings in battle and reformed his kingdom? Aethelflaed's father had defended his people of Wessex from a ruthless enemy, fighting his way back from exile to a crucial victory. He might not, as later generations believed, have either burned a peasant woman's cakes or spied on a Danish camp disguised as a minstrel. But he had contrived an effective defence system for Wessex and the adjoining kingdoms, promoted learning across Wessex, translated classic religious texts, founded abbeys and presided over a cosmopolitan court that welcomed scholars and other foreign visitors from across Western Europe. He took a keen interest in the upbringing of his children, his daughters as much as his sons, and particularly in that of Aethelflaed, his first-born. It was an upbringing that had to leave its mark.

Contrary to earlier received wisdom about the unique importance of strong mother figures as role models in a woman's development, recent research suggests that a daughter's self-confidence, ego strength and capacity for self-assertiveness depend greatly on positive guidance and encouragement from her father. Given the patriarchal structures predominant in most known societies, it is hardly surprising that a child, whether male or female, would look to the father rather than the mother for assurance and encouragement before taking action in the world.[140]

One important example Alfred set his daughter was that of personal courage. As a child she had witnessed his struggles for survival, and for the survival of his kingdom, in his most difficult time.

The flight to Athelney was not the first of Alfred's challenges. By the time Aethelflaed was 8 her father had been in battle – not counting minor skirmishes – at least sixteen times – at Nottingham, Reading, Ashdown, Basing, Wilton and Merton. In 870 alone, he fought in nine major engagements. In 874 he took to sea, leading a naval attack against incoming Vikings. He 'fought against seven ship-loads, and captured one of them and put the others to flight'.[141]

After his brother King Aethelred died in 871, Alfred succeeded him as king. He did so reluctantly, daunted by the military challenges ahead: 'for indeed he did not think that he alone could ever withstand such great ferocity of the Vikings, unless strengthened by divine help, since he had already sustained great losses of many men while his brothers were alive.'[142]

In spite of this seeming hesitancy in accepting the role of king, Alfred on the battlefield was remembered for bold decisive action – notably at Ashdown. Before the fight, while the Vikings were assembling their troops, he found that his older brother King Aethelred was still in his tent hearing Mass. Sizing up the situation – that the Vikings were gathering to begin the attack, Alfred had to make a quick decision – either to retreat, or engage with the enemy without the support of Aethelred. 'Like a wild boar', Bishop Asser writes, 'and strengthened by divine help ... he moved his army without delay against the enemy.' The day ended in victory for the Saxons.[143]

In her own experience of war, Alfred's daughter would have to make equally bold decisions – sending her army on a raid into Wales;

launching the attack on Derby. She chose personally to command her men in battle when faced with Viking incursions into Mercia – not a role any Saxon woman was expected to undertake. Moreover, she did it when already in her late thirties or early forties, an advanced age in early medieval times. In making these choices, she comes across as very much her father's daughter.

Equally bold was Aethelflaed's assumption, unheard-of in the Anglo-Saxon world, of the role of lone female ruler of a kingdom. At the most basic level, she was inheriting part of her father's responsibility for the government of Mercia, subject as the kingdom was to Wessex. Even if her task was shared with her husband during his lifetime, and with her brother Edward, heir to Alfred's throne, after Ealdorman Aethelred's death, she could have no illusions about the burdens, and the dangers, her position entailed.

Where did she learn to take such strides into the male adult world? Not only to ride into battle with a sword, but to govern a kingdom? Where did she gain the confidence? That confidence, which comes across to us as basic to Aethelflaed's personality, surely was acquired early in her life, and founded in childhood experience.

Often between a father and his eldest daughter there exists a special bond of trust and affection. The father feels pride in his child, especially if she is intelligent and capable. His daughter feels able to confide in him, and to learn from his experience of life. One likes to think Alfred experienced such pride in Aethelflaed as he watched her grow to womanhood; that he taught her, by example and by direct instruction, everything he knew. As she entered her teens, he might have talked to her about traditionally masculine things, like battlefield strategy and government; told her stories of his youth, perhaps, of his childhood visits to Rome; or of hunting expeditions with his friends as a young man, and of narrow escapes in battle. Perhaps he described to her how he allocated his wealth for the benefit of his kingdom; his plans for the church; the network of forts he hoped to see built across Wessex. How one day he hoped to win back Mercia from the Danes. Did he perhaps show her his workshops – the jewels he was designing for his craftsmen to make for him, or his blueprints for new buildings?

Though often characterised as 'neurotic' – and he suffered with a sense of sin that strikes many people as pathological – Alfred often showed a high degree of moral as well as physical courage. He persevered in resisting the Viking invasion even though, if we discount the rare victories before the battle of Edington, those years were mainly a catalogue of defeats. He led and protected his refugee community after the flight from Chippenham in 878, bringing eventual victory out of seemingly hopeless defeat. When he seemed to have lost everything – his throne, his lands, his reputation as protector of his people – almost his ability to feed his dependants – some quality of steady perseverance made it possible for him not only to survive and keep his immediate followers together, but to consolidate and build upon what small resources remained to him. It was this example to the people of Wessex that enabled him to gather an army that spring, and be welcomed back by those who might well have believed, up till then, that their king had abandoned them.

After Chippenham, and the flight to Athelney, the child Aethelflaed may well have shared her father's hardships. Under those grim conditions, living from hand to mouth in the fortress hidden in the frozen marshes, she would not only have picked up a range of practical survival skills, but had the opportunity to study how her father coped with adversity. She was to have her share of that in her own lifetime, as she struggled to shoulder the various burdens of a kingdom at war. When, after her husband's death, she found herself alone, with responsibility for the rule of Mercia, and Vikings on her doorstep, one likes to think she drew strength from her father's example.

'There is the most urgent necessity,' Alfred had written, 'occasionally to calm our minds amidst these earthly anxieties and direct them to divine and spiritual law ... to reflect on heavenly things amidst earthly tribulations.' Alfred believed that his quiet moments of religious devotion gave him clarity of insight – that from the wisdom gained from such moments one might learn, as he put it, 'caution, moderation, justice' – and 'courage'.[144] Alfred was apt to regard himself and his fellow human beings as merely visitors in this world, exiled from a native homeland beyond the earthly life. The task of each person, he believed – one that he took most seriously for himself – was 'to be useful here' on earth, but eventually 'to arrive there', in the spiritual realm 'whence you formerly came.' It was a message the devout father surely communicated to his children.[145]

Whether Aethelflaed felt herself sustained by personal religious devotion to the same degree as her father, we have no way of knowing. Her commitment to sustaining and endowing the physical fabric of the church through establishing buildings and shrines, though, was never in doubt; nor was the importance she and her husband ascribed to having prayers said for their souls after death.[146]

For Alfred it was both a religious and a secular duty to see that his people were properly educated, starting with himself. He often regretted aloud not having learned Latin as a boy, and the lack of competent tutors for him at that time: 'He would moan and sigh, lamenting bitterly,' Asser recalls, adding, 'He hopes others will do better at learning than himself.' In the Preface to his translation of Boethius's *Consolation of Philosophy*, Alfred asks readers 'not to blame him if they can interpret it more accurately than he was able'.[147]

It troubled Alfred that even those with minimal literacy in English were unable to understand Latin, the key not only to interpreting religious texts, but to dealing with law and government. Concerned that, in the aftermath of the Viking raids, few people south of the River Humber could even 'understand their divine services in English', or 'translate a single letter from Latin into English', the king famously assembled his group of scholars to undertake a translation project for the benefit of the people of Wessex. Like the early Christians in the Greek and Roman world who translated the Hebrew Bible into Greek and Latin, 'we too,' the king wrote, 'should turn into the language that we all can understand certain books which are the most necessary for all men to know'. These books included the Scriptures, Gregory's *Pastoral Care* (a volume of advice for those holding high office in the church), and the *Soliloquies* of St Augustine. Some of the translation work was done by Alfred himself, under the guidance of his scholarly team. The project was an act of restoration, an effort to recover for the church some of the treasure house of scholarship and learning that had existed before the disaster of the Viking invasions, 'before everything was ransacked and burned'.[148]

Aethelflaed's father believed that if religious education and scholarship were not promoted in the realm, its inhabitants would fail in Christian virtue. They would in time become 'Christians in name alone', and hence incur God's displeasure. 'Remember,' the king wrote, 'what punishments befell us in this world when we ourselves did not cherish learning, nor transmit it to other men.' (No doubt he had in mind his sufferings, and those of his subjects, at the hands of the Vikings.)

There is no explicit record of Aethelflaed performing any such services for ecclesiastical scholarship in Mercia as those of her father in Wessex, although as an educated woman herself, she surely would have agreed with her father that piety needed to be sustained by learning. She evidently saw to it, at least, that her daughter Aelfwynn and her nephew Athelstan, who was being raised at her court, received an appropriate education. We can assume that she aspired to a similar level of education for her two charges, to that which Alfred had required for his eldest child and her siblings. Whether she felt it important to extend education to others beyond the royal family, is unknown. Certainly, in seeing that her immediate family were taught well, she was following her father's example – preparing her young charges to be capable of playing a useful part in the running of a kingdom, as she herself was doing. Her chief contribution to cultural restoration, though – most famously in the construction of the 'Golden Minster' in Gloucester, and her building and restoration of other churches across Mercia – was carried out in wood and stone.

If, for Alfred, education was very much about religion, it was not for religion's sake to the exclusion of secular concerns. He wanted to build a better-educated society, to develop the capacities of the rising generation. His aspiration was for all 'free-born young men' with 'the means to apply themselves to it', who were not 'useful for some other employment' to learn to read English. (Latin too, if they aimed to join the priesthood.) He made a start with the children of nobles who were being trained at his court. He cherished these young people it is said, 'no less than his own children'. Alfred's youngest child Aethelweard was sent to the school his father founded, 'with all the nobly born children of ... the entire area, and a good many of lesser birth as well'.[149]

Sound educational policy has social implications, as Alfred was well aware. He sought to reduce miscarriages of justice that came about through the illiteracy and ignorance of his reeves, the judges who administered the law in Wessex at local level. The king is said to have required poorly educated reeves to brush up their Latin and study the law properly if they wanted to keep their jobs. Those who received these royal directives were 'terrified and chastened as if by the greatest of punishments', so that they made haste to improve their skills for fear of being turned out of office.[150] Whether or not Alfred's daughter ever imposed such a measure in her capacity as Lady of the Mercians, or even needed to, one feels that the no-nonsense approach would have appealed to her. One can certainly imagine her having a short way with ignorant judges – or with slovenly craftsmen or corrupt tax collectors, for that matter.

Her father was famously industrious and, above all, practical. Even his metaphor for literary composition is a practical one. Amassing material for a book, as he explains in a preface to his translation of Augustine's *Soliloquies*, entails assembling metaphorical 'staves and props and tie-shafts and handles', for fashioning each of the tools the writer wishes to use.[151] Alfred may have learned to handle actual tools in his youth. Certainly he enjoyed designing physical objects, from jewellery to buildings, 'marvellously constructed of stone and wood'. He devised a lantern with panes made of transparent ox horn, to keep the candles burning that he used to time his hours of prayer.[152] In 896 he commissioned new ships of a hybrid design, learning from examining captured Viking ships.[153] His daughter may not have built ships or designed jewellery, as far as we know, but she did share her father's enthusiasm for construction, for religious, military and civic purposes – not only commissioning buildings, but planning the layout of central streets in Mercian towns.

She seems to have been a believer in 'learning by doing'. When she wanted to train her daughter in the business of government, she involved her in the witnessing of legal documents while Aelfwynn was still in her teens. One could imagine Aethelflaed taking Aelfwynn with her to sessions of her witan, or to oversee building works, or to discuss a land grant with some ealdorman, to show her how things were done.[154]

Alfred loved system and organisational planning. He even employed his household on a shift system. Each contingent of royal officials gave a month of service at the court, followed by two months off. He carefully divided up his income, allocating various parts of his budget to different purposes. The Burghal Hidage, with its network of autonomously manned fortress towns, was originally his brainchild. Both Aethelflaed in Mercia, and her brother Edward in Wessex, respected their father's orderly approach to the burghal system, and carried out their father's programme to the letter. Aethelflaed worked particularly systematically, as we have seen, carefully securing the borders and other vulnerable points of her kingdom, before launching her attack on the Danelaw at Derby.

In his management of people – whether in appointing an abbot and his helpers for his new monastery at Athelney, or in assembling a translation team, or in his choice of a husband for Aethelflaed, Alfred thought equally systematically.[155] He deployed his daughters in marriage, if not like pawns on a chessboard, then much as he deployed men to command expeditions by his army.

Asser's *Life* offers some idea of Alfred's management style:

> *gently instructing, cajoling, urging, commanding, and (in the end, when his patience was exhausted) … sharply chastising those who were disobedient … by despising popular stupidity and stubbornness in every way, he*

94

carefully and cleverly exploited and converted his bishops and ealdormen and nobles, and his thegns most dear to him, and reeves as well … to his own will and to the general advantage of the whole realm.

Even when he knew that one of his judges, for instance, was grossly in the wrong, the king would begin by challenging him gently. He would ask politely, 'either in person or through one of his other trusted men', why they had 'passed so unfair a sentence …'. One can imagine the king's politeness being more unnerving than a reprimand.[156]

We get a glimpse of how tactful Alfred could be, in the preface to his translation of *Gregory's Pastoral Care*, where he calls on his bishops to use the new English translations of religious texts. 'Therefore it seems better to me,' the king writes '– if it seems so to you', that the books should be written 'in the language that we can all understand'. In the guise of a polite consultation lurks a royal command that the recipient would find hard to refuse.[157]

We know little about Aethelflaed's 'people skills', other than by inference. Like her father, though, she evidently inspired loyalty. To induce a conscript army to follow her into battle, in a time when conscripted men regularly voted with their feet if discontented, and to emerge victorious, or to get a burh the size of Warwick built in the space of a few months, suggests that she enjoyed her subjects' confidence, and that they rallied behind her.

She oversaw the day-to-day administration of a kingdom that by the end of her reign stretched from Gloucester to Runcorn, and from Leicester to the Welsh borders. Like Alfred, who kept a close eye on all that went on in his realm, from the building of new forts and the founding of abbeys, to the conduct of local courts, Aethelflaed stayed directly involved, personally overseeing a new burh project, or personally leading her army into battle.

Aethelflaed's father was known for his wide Continental connections, and for using them to the benefit of both Wessex and Mercia. The king not only recruited scholars and teachers, and foreign political allies, but even leaders from overseas for his new monasteries, when native Anglo-Saxons proved reluctant to enter the monastic life. Both commoners and members of royal families from across Western Europe pledged allegiance to Alfred, who was famed for his hospitality towards foreign visitors, regardless of their ethnic origins. 'Franks, Frisians, Gauls, Vikings, Welshmen, Irishmen, and Bretons … he ruled, loved, honoured and enriched them all with honour and authority.'[158]

Like Alfred, who corresponded with Rome, and built an alliance with the Franks against Viking raiders, his equally broad-minded daughter reached out beyond the borders of her kingdom. When Aethelflaed inherited the rule of Mercia in 911, she established a tradition of wide-ranging diplomacy, engaging with neighbouring rulers in mutual defence. She was far more adventurous in this respect, than her husband had been. She had an ability to form strong alliances with her neighbours – and even, when it appeared the time was right, with former enemies. Her skill in foreign relations could have been learned from Alfred, along with what we in modern terms would call an internationalist attitude – a product of her upbringing at Alfred's cosmopolitan court.

In so much she did, from founding new churches to launching the offensive to win back Derby from the Danes, from rebuilding Gloucester to engaging with Viking peace overtures from York, Aethelflaed comes across as bold, radical, and very independent. Obliged to function within patriarchal structures, in the last analysis she refused to be an acolyte of any of the dominant males who surrounded her – not of her husband or her brother (though she cooperated closely with both of them), and certainly not of her father.

Aethelflaed was not only Alfred's eldest daughter, but his eldest child. She would have enjoyed her father's undivided attention for some years before the next child, Edward, was old enough to be of much interest to him. A daughter is greatly empowered by the absence of brothers – rendered more likely to envisage non-traditional or traditionally 'masculine' leadership roles for herself in adult life. Women who have grown up without a brother are said to be 'overly represented' among the world's female political leaders, thanks to the greater degree of support and encouragement they tend to receive from their fathers.[159]

If, as some historians have suggested, there existed a certain amount of tension between Aethelflaed and her brother Edward as adults, sibling rivalry may have played its part. Edward had grown up in the shadow of a favoured daughter, while Aethelflaed might have resented her brother for the increasing share of her father's attention he would have received as he grew older. To find herself compelled to work with that younger brother, overlord of her sub-kingdom of Mercia after Alfred's death, must have been difficult.[160]

A favoured daughter who carries on the work of a famous political father, is not an unfamiliar phenomenon in the modern world. Indira Gandhi, daughter of India's first prime minister Jawaharlal Nehru, and later head of government in her own right; Megawati Sukarnoputri, whose father was Indonesia's first president after independence, and the country's only female president to date; Aung San Suu Kyi of Burma, all echo the relationship that, I suggest, shaped the identity and powers of Alfred's eldest child.

Like her father, Aetheflaed wished 'to live worthily', and to leave behind her a memory of herself in good works.[161] Like him, she would leave a material legacy to the world. Where Alfred, however, wrote of being remembered by 'the men who should come after' him, his daughter broadened the conception of her legacy to encompass at least one woman – her only child, Aelfwynn. Was it the confidence that came from her upbringing that enabled Aethelflaed to take the unheard-of step of providing for her daughter to succeed her on the throne of Mercia?

CHAPTER SEVEN

Aethelflaed's (Missing) Daughter

'To hear her described as "queen" must have made her brother very nervous.'[162]

After years of military struggle to contain the Viking threat, Aethelflaed in 918 was on the brink of a political triumph. When she besieged the Viking-held town of Leicester, it surrendered to her army without a fight, and 'the most part of the raiding-armies' based in the town, were 'brought under her control.'[163] Better still, from Aethelflaed's point of view, was what happened next. The surrender at Leicester was followed by the arrival at Tamworth of emissaries from the kingdom of York, centre of Viking power in the northern Danelaw. The leading citizens in York wished to submit themselves to the rule of Mercia, to swear allegiance to Aethelflaed as their 'overlord'. They would, they assured her, 'be at her disposition'. Finally, it seemed, after years of turmoil and misery, the kingdom of Mercia might look forward to a period of peace. The surrender of York to Mercian rule would have been a triumph for Aethelflaed. If the pact had been finalised, it would have meant not only an increase in her personal power, but prosperity and security for the people of Mercia as a whole.

The news of an impending deal between Mercia and York would not have been welcome, however at the court in Wessex. In fact it probably caused consternation. King Edward was still engaged in an increasingly successful war to bring the East Anglian territories of the Danelaw back under Saxon control. Soon he would take the fight northwards. Aethelflaed's impending treaty with the Danes in

York would complicate these plans. Worse, from Edward's point of view, was the huge increase in power for Mercia that the deal implied. A resurgent Mercia, no longer a sub-realm of Wessex but an independent kingdom in its own right with York as its dependent, was an alarming prospect. Mercia could even threaten to become, as it had been in the past, a rival to Wessex itself.

Arguably, the implications of the threatened treaty were, for Edward, not only political, but also personal. The tensions, ever latent in the relationship of brother and sister, were rising to the surface.[164]

Edward's nightmare never came to pass. Before York's formal submission could be received, an unexpected event intervened. In June the Lady of the Mercians suddenly died. It happened, the *Anglo-Saxon Chronicles* tell us, 'very quickly'. She 'departed ... before midsummer, inside Tamworth.'[165]

A year later, the Norse leader Raegnald, a formidable warlord, opposed by those who had sought protection from Aethelflaed, came to power in York. Another nine years would go by, before Aethelflaed's nephew Athelstan – having unsuccessfully tried to broker a treaty with Raegnald's successor – would subdue the northern Danelaw by the sword.

Aethelflaed's death at this crucial moment seems almost too coincidental. It might be tempting to speculate whether foul play was involved in her sudden demise – if not involving Wessex, then from some faction in the kingdom of York opposed to the Danish submission to Mercia. For over two decades, though, Aethelflaed had lived strenuously, on the battlefield and off it. In the last seven years of her life, or possibly for longer, she had shouldered the burdens, physical and psychological, of ruling Mercia alone. In 918 she would have been in her late forties – old, by early medieval standards. (Her father Alfred had died at fifty. Edward would outlive his sister by just six years.) Possibly Aethelflaed succumbed to a stroke or a heart attack, brought on by age and exhaustion. In any case, it is quite likely that she died of natural causes.

She collapsed, surrounded by attendants who rushed to help her to bed. People crowded about her – ladies in waiting, menservants,

Aelfwynn her daughter. (Was Aethelstan, too, sent for?) A priest was summoned. He heard her final, barely audible, confession. He administered the last rites. Everyone watched anxiously, helplessly, as she slipped away into unconsciousness. Aethelflaed, Lady of the Mercians, had ended her earthly life.

Her body was carried southwards through Mercia. People of all ranks stood by the roadside as the funeral carriage, guarded by her thegns and other men who had fought with her in battle, went by. They knelt and crossed themselves, heads bowed, as it passed. By boat, the coffin was borne down the Severn from Worcester to its last resting place, the minster of St Oswald that Aethelflaed and Aethelred had founded together. Aethelflaed's remains were laid there beside her husband's, in the separate mausoleum built for them, a freestanding crypt at the east end of the church. An ornately carved stone slab found at St Oswald's, now in Gloucester's city museum, may once have covered her grave.

In Worcester, the clergy of St Peter's would, as she had requested, recite the Laudate Dominum daily for her, and say a mass every Saturday for her and her husband's souls.[166]

What would happen now, people were asking themselves, as the news spread across Mercia that the powerful woman who had been a fixture in their lives for over thirty years, was gone. Her rule had brought them prosperity and stability. Now that stability seemed less assured. Who would, or could, replace their Lady of the Mercians?

It would have been unlikely Aethelflaed to have left no answer to this question. Although her will has not survived, and contemporary chronicles tell us nothing either, the smoothness of the initial transition to power after her death suggests that she had explicitly named her daughter Aelfwynn as her successor.

As we know, Aethelflaed had involved Aelfwynn in affairs of government from an early age. The daughter witnessed charters while still in her early teens. A land grant, made under Edward's jurisdiction, bears Aelfwynn's signature, and also the Worcester charter of 904, leasing land in the town to Aethelred and Aethelflaed. (In the latter document, Aelfwynn is named as her parents' heir to that land:

'Æthelred and Æthelflæd shall hold it for all time, both within the town wall and without, uncontested by anyone as long as they live. And if Ælfwynn survives them, it shall similarly remain uncontested as long as she lives'.[167])

If Aethelflaed, as a lone female ruler was remarkable in the history of Anglo-Saxons in England up to that point, for another woman to succeed her on the throne was more extraordinary still. Yet the Mercian witan apparently accepted Aelfwynn as the new Lady of the Mercians without controversy. They already knew and trusted her and had faith in her mother's choice. Nothing, it seemed, could prevent Aelfwynn from carrying on in power as her mother had done before her.

Over the border in Wessex though, other plans were forming. Eighteen months after Aelfwynn had begun her reign as the new Lady of the Mercians, her uncle Edward arrived in Tamworth at the head of an army, and forced his niece from power.

If we believe the entry in the *Anglo-Saxon Chronicles*, as composed in the Wessex royal capital of Winchester, this was just what the Mercians had all been waiting for and they welcomed Edward as their ruler: 'All the nation of the land of Mercia, which earlier was subject to Aethelflaed', is said to have welcomed Aelfwynn's uncle Edward as a better choice than Aethelflaed's daughter, and 'turned to him'.[168]

The Mercian version known as the Mercian Register, tells a rather different story. When Edward arrived at Tamworth, the narrative tells us bluntly, 'The daughter of Aethelred, lord of the Mercians, was deprived of all dominion over the Mercians, and carried into Wessex.'[169] The wording of this version, with its connotations of violation – 'deprived', 'carried' – speaks eloquently to us. But so, by its omissions, does the account from Winchester, with Edward's triumphant arrival in Tamworth. In the Winchester narrative, the deposing of Aelfwynn, and even Aelfwynn's name, go unmentioned. It is as if her brief reign had never been. The very silence about the second Lady of the Mercians, speaks volumes.

The Welsh chronicler Caradoc, an admirer of the military prowess of Aelfwynn's mother, is indignant over the fate of her daughter. After the death of Aethelflaed, he says, King Edward 'most ungratefully' disinherited Aelfwynn. Caradoc is in no doubt that Edward unlawfully invaded the kingdom of Mercia and annexed it: 'Entering into Mercia', he 'took all the province into his own hands'.[170]

'Ungratefully' is an interesting word here. Presumably Caradoc was thinking of Aethelflaed's unflaggingly loyal support of her brother in resisting the Viking threat – a commitment to which she had given her whole adult life. Surely, Caradoc implies, the Lady of the Mercians deserved more as her legacy after death than having her only child unceremoniously evicted from the Mercian throne?

What did the Mercian people make of Edward's sudden brutal intervention in their affairs? They were shocked, no doubt. But Edward was, after all, Mercia's overlord. Mercian sovereignty had, for the thirty-three years since King Alfred first appointed Aethelred to govern London, been at the discretion of the royal house of Wessex.

It has been suggested that Edward met with the Mercian witan before removing Aelfwynn from power, that in fact he deposed her with their consent. But if he met with the witan at all, it was less likely to have been to consult them, than to give them an order – one enforceable by the army at his back. The witan would do the bidding of the ruler of Wessex as their overlord. And who was Aelfwynn, after all? Without her royal mother to uphold her claim, she was merely the daughter of an ealdorman, and a deceased one at that.[171]

Aelfwynn was, moreover, as much subject as any peasant woman, to the patriarchal Wessex laws that governed family ties. With both her parents dead, her uncle Edward was now her next of kin, and stood in the relation of a father to her – a very powerful one, with his own political agenda.

Caradoc states that Aelfwynn's mother had formally appointed Edward as her daughter's 'guardian'. While this seems unlikely in any formal sense – Aelfwynn must have been in her thirties when Aethelflaed died, and was obviously regarded as capable of assuming the rule of a kingdom – still, Wessex cultural norms held male kin responsible towards, and as having rights over, female relatives. Women were subject to these patriarchal norms even after they married, and certainly in cases where they remained single.[172]

AETHELFLAED'S (MISSING) DAUGHTER

What was happening to Aelfwynn was not actually so unusual. It was fairly common for any new Anglo-Saxon ruler to face a challenge to his leadership. There was no strict law of dynastic succession in the Anglo-Saxon kingdoms – one reason why challenges to the authority of a new ruler happened so often. Aelfwynn's great-grandfather Aethelwulf had returned to Wessex after a trip to Rome to find his treacherous son Aethelbald trying to replace him as king. Edward, in the early months of his reign, had faced down a challenge from his cousin Aethelwold. Edward's own son Athelstan, when his turn came to rule, would face a similar threat. Even before the Vikings seized control and installed their puppet king, the kingdom of Mercia had lurched from one succession crisis to another. If no one had seriously tried to depose King Alfred, it may have been that no one wanted the unenviable job at that historical moment of fending off hordes of seemingly invincible Vikings. (Unless of course, we accept the theory that treachery was involved in driving Alfred and his family out of Chippenham in 878; in which case, he too had problems with challenges from ambitious rivals. Certainly Alfred in the later years of his reign in Wessex, was careful to require loyalty oaths from all his dependants and kin, and to specify in his will that Edward was to reign after him.) If Aethelflaed had lived a little longer, she might have been better able to ease her daughter's transition into power; but that was not to be.

Apart from the fear of resurgent Mercian independence, could there have been any other reason why Edward was so eager to remove his niece from power? Was Aelfwynn, for instance, proving herself unfit to rule in some way? If so, there is no record of it. All we know is that she lacked sufficient toughness to stand up to her ruthless and powerful uncle Edward. Given a similar challenge, her mother would have been a better match for him. It's difficult to imagine Aethelflaed allowing herself to be dethroned and carried off from her own palace, without at least trying to put up some resistance. Indeed one doubts that, if confronted with his formidable sister, rather than her inexperienced and vulnerable daughter, Edward would have made the abduction attempt in the first place.

Caradoc has a further interesting suggestion as to why Edward found it necessary to depose his niece. Edward, he says, accused Aelfwynn of secretly arranging a marriage between herself and Raegnald, the new Viking ruler of York. In Caradoc's view this was simply Edward's pretext for removing her from power: 'upon pretence that she, without his knowledge … had privily promised and contracted marriage with Raynald King of the Danes'. For Caradoc, no such marriage plan existed; it was all a ruse on King Edward's part. But what if Aelfwynn, in a bid to carry on the peace negotiations with the kingdom of York begun by her mother, really *had* made such a contract with the new Viking leader? If in fact Aelfwynn really had aimed, through marriage, to build a new powerful alliance of York with Mercia, to the benefit of both kingdoms? Knowing how alarming Edward would find the news of any such alliance in the making – one that categorically did not include Wessex – Aelfwynn would certainly have wanted to be discreet about her plans. Given Aethelflaed's previous involvement with York, and the aborted treaty with the Danes that had remained unsigned at her death, Edward's accusation actually seems quite plausible.[173]

One might wonder why Aelfwynn had in any case remained unwed for so long? Unless destined for the convent, a young woman was normally married off by her parents while still in her mid-teens at the latest – usually to a husband who would benefit her family, either economically or politically. If she was destined to rule Mercia after her mother's death, however, Aelfwynn's continuing single state makes more sense. Any marriage with some member of a ruling elite – a Saxon almost as much as a Dane – would tend to compromise her independence as Lady of the Mercians. Her mother's position had been secured by the fact that Ealdorman Aethelred was his wife's social inferior, and because the marriage was backed and overseen by King Alfred at the height of his power.

It may be that Edward genuinely regarded any proposed match between a Mercian ruler and a Viking leader as foolhardy and dangerous, bringing with it the risk that the husband might become the dominant political partner in the relationship. Certainly it was something he could have alleged, as Caradoc suggests, to justify an action he had been contemplating all along. Aelfwynn's stupidity, he might have told himself, had to be thwarted. Suspicion of the intended marriage may have been the catalyst that, after allowing Aelfwynn to reign for nearly eighteen months, finally provoked him to depose her.[174]

Yet another possible source of conflict between Aethelflaed and her brother may have been the future of Edward's son Athelstan. Had it perhaps been agreed between Edward and Aethelflaed – or at least tacitly understood – that Athelstan, rather than Aelfwynn, would succeed Aethelflaed as ruler of Mercia? We are told that Athelstan had been singled out for favour by Alfred his grandfather, who honoured him with gifts of a purple cloak, and a sword in a golden scabbard. Did Edward believe, correctly or otherwise, that his son had been cheated of his right?[175]

After forcing Aelfwynn from power, Edward assumed direct rule over Mercia, and renewed the war with the Danelaw. Having seized back Nottingham from Danish control, he travelled on up north with a conscript army of Mercians, to strengthen fortifications at Manchester.

Whether Edward's decision to govern Mercia from his kingdom of Wessex was as universally popular as the Winchester version of the *Anglo-Saxon Chronicles* suggests, is open to question. The Wessex royal centre at Winchester must have seemed a long way from Tamworth. Five years after his deposition of Aelfwynn, the people of Chester rose in revolt against Edward. They apparently regarded the king of Wessex as little better than a foreign invader. He was obliged to ride north to suppress the rebellion. He garrisoned the city with his own loyal troops, and had to make concessions to the Chester citizens, relieving them of traditional obligations of bridge restoration, and remitting some of their taxes.[176]

Shortly after subduing the rebellion, Edward died at Farndon on Dee, seven miles from Chester. His son Aelfweard, his chosen heir to the throne of Wessex, died just fifteen days later. Athelstan was acclaimed as king of both Wessex and Mercia, including by the Mercian nobles, without controversy. He was, after all, well known in Mercia. Probably the Mercians preferred to be subject to Athelstan rather than to a stranger from Wessex.

Before his ride into Mercia to seize control, having his son Athelstan rule the Mercians may have been Edward's aim all along. It was Athelstan who, in a series of bloody battles, would complete the unification of what became the nation of England, bringing all the Anglo-Saxon kingdoms, as well as the former Danelaw, under his single rule. All the same, to anyone aware of the abrupt end to the short reign of Aelfwynn, it will seem a little ironic that the well-known statue of Aethelflaed at Tamworth represents the Lady of the Mercians with her arm around Athelstan, rather than Aelfwynn, her chosen successor in Mercia – presumably because Athelstan was the first king of all England.[177]

To return to Aelfwynn: what became of her, after she was so unceremoniously removed from power?

One may imagine her – no longer Lady of the Mercians, but merely Aelfwynn, daughter of Aethelred – riding southward out of Tamworth, along roads travelled by her mother's funeral cortege just months before. The horse trotting briskly, one of Edward's thegns holding it tightly on a leading rein. Armed men surround Aelfwynn, a moving wall of helmets and spears. Furious at the indignity of this kidnapping, sharply conscious of the injustice of it, she frets, too, about the duties she has been forced to abandon; pledges and commitments left unfulfilled. Is apprehensive, too, no doubt, on her own account. What fate does her uncle Edward have in mind for her?

She disappears into Wessex now, and out of history.

The favourite theory among historians as to what became of Aelfwynn, is that she ended up in some nunnery – the usual destination of women whose families, for whatever reason, found them surplus to requirements. There, she might live out her days in reasonable physical comfort, and be kept under surveillance by members of the royal house of Wessex. The name Aelfwynn does in fact appear in a list of 'distinguished women' ('Nomina Feminarum Illustrium'), compiled at the Nunnaminster in Winchester in 1031. The religious house founded by Aelfwynn's maternal grandmother Ealhswith is a not unlikely place for Aelfwynn to have been taken. But the name could also refer to the sister of the abbot who compiled the list. The evidence is hardly conclusive.[178]

AETHELFLAED'S (MISSING) DAUGHTER

In telling of the abduction of Aelfwynn and her likely subsequent fate, historians tend to wax consoling. Aelfwynn may have been detained in a convent, but she came to no real harm. One feminist historian goes so far as to claim that Aelfwynn's deposition from the throne of Mercia, 'ultimately provided her with a modicum of safety', and a refuge in the 'vibrant female community' of a convent. Was safety a priority for the daughter of Aethelflaed, a woman who had lived her own life in the thick of danger? Who, in any case, would welcome 'safety' at the price of enduring preventive detention? The same writer questions whether 'royal parents, especially mothers', really want their children to succeed to the throne in a continuation of the patriarchal order. Aethelflaed devoted over twenty years to training her daughter for public life, and after her mother's death Aelfwynn accepted the title of Lady of the Mercians as of right. To discover that Aethelflaed really wanted 'a different sort of success' for her daughter, all along – the safety of a nunnery, perhaps? – would be strange indeed.[179]

It was not until the sixteenth century, and the consecutive reigns of Mary Tudor and Elizabeth I, that one woman would succeed another as a monarch in England. In this respect, Aelfwynn was a pioneer. That is, admittedly, a modest claim to fame, one that speaks more, perhaps, for the radical vision of Aelfwynn's mother, than for Aelfwynn herself. If the daughter had been allowed a chance to prove herself in power, however, instead of being arbitrarily deposed and kidnapped, who knows what she might have achieved?

In the unending round of prayers and vigils, the long sessions with heads bent silent over sewing, or listening to readings from the Church Fathers; in the brief snatches of sleep that convent routine allowed, did Aelfwynn's mind fill with images of a different time? Presiding at a session of her witan. Welcoming her guests to the palace at Kingsholm, garlanded with green boughs for Christmas. At Runcorn, standing on the fortress wall built by her mother, looking out across the gleaming expanse of the Mersey. Or on the Severn marshes, on horseback, gazing upward to catch sight of her falcon returning, circling above her in the open sky.

CHAPTER EIGHT

Legend and Legacy

'of equal service in building cities'
'able to protect men at home, and to intimidate them abroad'.
'She definitively kicked Viking butt at the battle of Tettenhall.'
'Unconquerable queen, farewell!' [180]

Defender and protector of her people; heroic, and sometimes ruthless, warrior; companion, wife; dutiful daughter; ambitious mother; rival sibling; 'queen'; patron of the church; strategist and diplomat; capable administrator; founder of cities. Which of these many Aethelflaeds should, today in the early twenty-first century, be singled out to define her? Which of these roles are we to view as constituting her abiding legacy?

The answers to these questions have shifted over the centuries. This book has been an attempt to address various aspects of Aethelflaed; the roles she came to play at different times, in terms of what we know about the Lady of the Mercians and the society she lived in – to understand the forces that shaped her personality and her life.

It is generally agreed that the *Anglo-Saxon Chronicles*, a crucial source for understanding the history of King Alfred and his dynasty are, with the exception of the Mercian Register section, told largely from the point of view of Wessex and the court at Winchester, with a general disregard of affairs in Mercia. Aethelflaed's brother, moreover, and his male descendants who ruled after him had no interest in keeping the story of Aethelflaed's achievements alive. Edward's treatment of her daughter, and his subjugation of Mercia under direct rule from Wessex, meant that the less said about the two women who had ruled the kingdom before he claimed it as his own, the better.

The Norman conquest of England, and the massive building programme that followed it in the twelfth century, made for a general erasure of Anglo-Saxon cultural landmarks. Towns came to be dominated by forbidding castles that upstaged the more modest fortifications of the Anglo-Saxon burhs. (The latter, unlike the Norman castles, were designed to preserve the community as a whole, rather than the safety of a single lord and his family. They were 'for the protection of all the people'.) Saxon churches were replaced by impressive stone buildings on the original site, cancelling out the memory of their founding. Often the church was re-dedicated in the name of a new saint, so that even the religious traditions once connected with it were forgotten. And Aethelflaed's part in its founding was forgotten too.

Among those who have chosen to remember Aetheflaed's legacy, the focus has most often centred on her achievements either as a female warrior, as a ruler in a time when women were not expected to govern, or as the founder of the towns of the Midlands, through her construction of the burhs. These three aspects of her life, and her reputation and image among succeeding generations, are what will mainly be considered here.

There have been long periods when questions about Aethelflaed and her legacy have ceased to be asked at all, when the Lady of the Mercians all but vanished from collective memory. Her image is returning now to public awareness – in the pages of academic histories and romantic novels, but also in more surprising places: on the Internet, for example, in ads for cosmetics and beer; in commemorative plaques on town walls and the sculptures erected in public squares. The image remains a shifting one, focusing on diverse facets of her achievements.

Some twenty-first century representations of Aethelflaed are ones her contemporaries would not have recognised. Chiefly, though, as in her own time, her modern chroniclers tend to celebrate one of two key aspects: the unconventional role she played as a female warrior, or her work of building and founding towns and churches.

For the anonymous narrator(s) who composed the Mercian pages of the *Anglo-Saxon Chronicles*, Aethelflaed's achievements are almost exclusively military. (The *Chronicles* as a whole are of course largely concerned with narrating the overall struggle against Viking invasion.) The Mercian Register entries record her victories at Brecon Mere and Derby, the subjugation of the Danes of Leicester, and the building of burhs for military defence. They have little to say about her founding of churches, her endowment of religious shrines, her diplomatic activities, or her overall administration of Mercia.

The *Fragmentary Annals of Ireland*, compiled in the late tenth or early eleventh century, likewise emphasise Aethelflaed's military prowess, in particular her defence of Chester, and her victory over the Viking leader Oittir. Her skill in diplomacy gets a brief mention, in describing her wartime alliances with the men of Alba and others, against Norwegian invaders. The twelfth-century Welsh chronicler Caradoc also stresses Aethelflaed's military role in her victory at Derby, and her incursions into Wales. He describes Aethelflaed's fortifying of towns and castles in this strategic context – 'against the incursions of the Danes'. She was, Caradoc writes, a woman 'of singular virtues', who 'greatly strengthened the kingdom of Mercia' by providing it with secure means of defence. These military accomplishments, it seems, were what mattered to many who lived nearest her own time.[181]

That she was a queen in her own right, the Irish had no doubt. 'Famosissima regina' – most famous queen – the *Annals of Ulster* compiled in the late fifteenth century called her, recalling her death as the most significant event of 918.[182]

She was certainly not forgotten in popular memory by many living closer to her own time. The peoples of Mercia and Wessex celebrated Aethelflaed by giving her name to their children – rather as families named their sons Washington or Jefferson after the Founding Fathers of the United States. Before it was given to Alfred's daughter, the name Aethelflaed was not common. After the Lady of the Mercians, there were quite a few Aethelflaeds in high-status families (and possibly some in families of less exalted standing, where records have been lost to us).

Known Aethelflaeds after 918:

Aethelflaed of Damerham, daughter of Ealdorman Aelfar of Essex. (She became the second wife of King Edmund I, who reigned from 939 to 946.)

Aethelflaed Eneda, who married King Edgar, 'The Peaceful' (reigned from 959 to 975).

Aethelflaed, daughter of Ealdorman Ealhhelm, who was an ealdorman in Mercia in the mid-tenth century. Like Aethelred, the husband of the Lady of the Mercians, Ealhhelm had connections to the Hwicce people of southwestern Mercia. An older relative is said to have served the Lady of the Mercians as an ealdorman, so no doubt family loyalties were involved in Ealhhelm's choice of the name.

Aethelflaed, mother of Ealdorman Aethelmaer, whose son was born to her in 960.

Aethelflaed, daughter of a woman named Wynflaed, to whom she bequeathed clothing in her will, Wynflaed mentions a second Aethelflaed, nicknamed 'The White'. That there were two Aethelflaeds in the same close-knit community suggests how common the name had become.[183]

Were these women so named because their parents admired Aethelflaed's heroic strength of character? Or was it because people remembered that she had fought to save them from the Vikings?

Writing in the twelfth century, Henry of Huntingdon, courtier and would-be poet, likewise enthused about Aethelflaed's military prowess. His no doubt well-intentioned Latin verse in her honour offers a somewhat backhanded compliment:

> *O potent Elfleda! Maid, men's terror!*
> *You did conquer nature's self; worthy*
> *The name of man! More beauteous nature's form of*
> *A woman; but your valour shall secure*
> *Man's higher name. For name you only need*
> *Not sex to change; unconquerable queen,*
> *King rather, who such trophies have obtained!*

O virgin and virago both farewell!
No Caesar yet such triumph hath deserved.
As you, than any, all, the Caesars more renown'd! [184]

Henry of Huntingdon is fascinated with Aethelflaed's martial achievements, and with her heroism as a warrior – achievements and traits he clearly regards as normally the prerogative of men. Her martial prowess has, he claims, conquered her inferior female nature, making her worthy of 'man's higher name'. (Not bad for a girl!) Curiously, perhaps unaware that Aethelflaed had a daughter, he also refers to her as 'virgin'. This would be one way of insisting on her sexual virtue, while linking her implicitly with some virgin goddess of antiquity, such as Artemis. He overlooks the complexity of Aethelflaed's status in another important way, when he claims that her triumphs exceeded those of a 'Caesar'. Aethelflaed, unlike most of the Roman emperors, took to the battlefield not primarily from a desire for conquest, but in defence of her kingdom, when warfare was forced upon her

Other medieval representations offer a broader perspective than Henry of Huntingdon's poem. A more nuanced tribute appears in another twelfth-century work, William of Malmesbury's *Chronicle of the Kings of England*:

> *And here indeed Ethelfled, sister of the king and relict of Ethered, ought not to be forgotten, as she was a powerful accession to his party, the delight of his subjects, the dread of his enemies, a woman of an enlarged soul ... This spirited heroine assisted her brother greatly with her advice, was of equal service in building cities, nor could you easily discern, whether it was more owing to fortune or her own exertions, that a woman should be able to protect men at home, and to intimidate them abroad.* [185]

William sees that Aethelflaed was more than a courageous warrior – that she was a protector of her community, and a builder – 'of equal service in building cities'. He acknowledges her intelligence, and that she probably 'assisted her brother ... with her advice'. At the same time, he struggles to understand her – being, as we have seen, particularly puzzled as to why she bore only one child, and a daughter at that. He can, moreover, think of the Lady of the Mercians only within a patriarchal framework – as Edward's sister, Aethelred's 'relict' (widow). He thinks of her work in the world primarily in terms of its usefulness to Edward, to whom she was 'a powerful accession'. And how could a mere woman achieve as she did? Was it through force of character, through 'her own exertions' – or merely 'owing to fortune' that she accomplished so much? Perhaps her 'enlarged soul' had something to do with it – meaning that she was more like a man, and hence superior to the rest of her sex?

The phenomenon of a female ruler was not one wholly outside William's experience. Indeed it has been argued that William's portrait of Aethelflaed is designed to celebrate and legitimise the rule of a powerful female contemporary – Matilda, his patron's sister, who was fighting to regain the throne of England from her usurping cousin Stephen.[186]

Whether or not William of Malmesbury's portrait of Aethelflaed is intended to flatter Matilda, he certainly acknowledges the full range of Aethelflaed's abilities and accomplishments – not least in 'building cities'.

While no one knows what Aethelflaed looked like, several medieval images of her exist. These are mostly quite conventional stereotypes of a female ruler on royal genealogies and other documents. Within these conventions, however, we see that in the later Middle Ages Aethelflaed was, once again, appreciated for more than simply her military prowess. The representations may be formulaic, but they differ distinctively from one another. A thirteenth-century cartulary (a collection of copies of charters) from Abingdon Abbey shows a dignified woman wearing a simple crown and draped in a blue mantle, seated on a cushioned throne. In her right hand she holds a sceptre, while her left hand is lifted, palm upwards, as if making some declaration, or issuing a judgment. This Aethelflaed is far away from the battlefield, performing her day-to-day functions as administrator of a kingdom.[187]

One thirteenth-century genealogy, quite surprisingly, depicts Aethelflaed as a pale nun-like figure robed all in white, whose right hand is raised to touch what seems to be a crucifix hanging around her neck. ('La Sage' – The Wise – runs the caption above her head). The image is so remote from anything we might expect of the Lady of the Mercians, that one has to wonder if the artist has not confused Aethelflaed with her younger sister Aethelgifu, abbess of Shaftesbury.[188]

Another genealogy, from a hundred years later, also presents us with 'La Sage' Aethelflaed. This one wears a fourteenth-century headdress, her hair bound up with nets, with a ribbon under her chin. Her face appears in a three-quarter view, the eyes looking to the side with a half-smile on her lips, that gives her an intelligent, knowing appearance. This Aethelflaed would be most comfortable in deliberations with her counsellors, or working out an alliance with some neighbouring ruler.[189]

For more than five centuries, Aethelflaed vanishes both from official records, and from popular legend. Even when interest in the Anglo-Saxons' legacy becomes intense in England in the seventeenth century, it is animated by the religious and political ideals of the Reformation and the English Civil War, and the imagined founding contributions of King Alfred to institutions such as trial by jury, rather than by an interest in Anglo-Saxon history in general. Scholars like John Spelman, author of a highly influential seventeenth-century *Life of Alfred the Great*, promoted the idealised, and largely erroneous, myth of a free society under Alfred's enlightened rule. According to this version, Alfred helped to found a constitutional monarchy – until the oppressive 'Norman yoke' fell upon England. It had been possible to translate the Scriptures into English, as the king himself had done, without fear of being burned alive as a heretic. Then, in this inaccurate account of Alfred's reign – he did not in fact introduce jury trials, or extend democracy – William the Conqueror arrived in England and subjugated the 'free Anglo-Saxon people'.[190]

There was little room in this mythical version of Anglo-Saxondom for an Aethelflaed. As warrior princess, or as builder of cities, let alone as a feminist icon, she simply did not fit the picture.

After centuries of silence, Aethelflaed makes a brief appearance again – as a warrior heroine in an anonymous play of the eighteenth century. *Alfred the Great; deliverer of his country* (1753), portrays King Alfred's resistance to the Vikings at Athelney. In this highly fictionalised version of Anglo-Saxon history, Aethelflaed ('Elfleda') fights alongside her Ethelred, 'Firmly resolved to share all dangers', with her beloved. Captured by a Viking leader and threatened with rape, she draws a hidden dagger, and stabs her attacker. 'O! Most heroic, charming, matchless Princess,' exclaims Ethelred, when he learns what she has done. In a brief facetious Epilogue to the play, the actress playing Elfleda defends her right to do battle alongside her menfolk:

> *Dames of old*
> *Would quit their petticoats, and put on Breeches*
> *Or risk their lives ... they were cunning Witches.*
> *Breeches they wore, and very oft wou'd rent 'em;*
> *And who, besides their Husbands, wou'd prevent 'em?*[191]

The representation of Alfred's daughter overlooks the fact that Aethelflaed was a child at the time of the Athelney episode. But it offers something of a proto-feminist view, even if an implausible and sometimes facetious one, of a woman ready to risk her life in battle. Again, as so often in representations of Aethelflaed, it is the idea of the female warrior that takes precedence over her other achievements.

The anonymous dramatist knows about Aethelflaed, as he tells us, from an English translation of the contemporary French historian Paul de Rapin, who in turn can be seen to derive his information mainly from the twelfth-century chroniclers – chiefly William of Malmesbury. De Rapin adds nothing new to these earlier texts. Aethelflaed, he writes, distinguished herself by her 'Manlike and Royal Abilities'. She fortified towns, and 'obliged the Welsh to become her Tributaries'.[192] His brief account of Aethelflaed's achievements is remarkable mainly because it indicates that she was still sometimes remembered in historical accounts as late as the early eighteenth century.

To the Victorian understanding of the Anglo-Saxon world, on the other hand, the cult of Aethelflaed's father was what mattered. The late nineteenth century saw a wholesale fascination with Anglo-Saxon England and its culture, at least partly driven by the nationalistic pride of citizens of the British Empire. The Anglo-Saxon language was referred to as 'Old English', emphasising its continuity with modern English, and the roots of English 'greatness' in the Anglo-Saxon past. Academic translation of Anglo-Saxon texts became a national industry. In the popular imagination, the idea of Anglo-Saxon achievement continued to be centred around a single figure, that of King Alfred. The millenary of Alfred's death, celebrated in 1901, two years after the king's actual demise – grew from small beginnings in Winchester into a national event, with military parades, unveiling of statues, the participation of learned academics, and the launching of a new warship named after the Saxon king. (Alfred was mistakenly believed to have founded the British navy.)

The millenary was an almost all-male event, organised by all-male committees of the great and the good. It focused, quite understandably, on Alfred's victories over the Danes. (It was his anniversary, after all.) Even in dramatic representations of the events of the king's life, Anglo-Saxon women were scarcely represented. They did appear in a tableau staged at Winchester, as nurses – 'Saxon women attending the wounded'. They looked like nuns – 'pristine, heavily wimpled and angelic'. Another tableau represented women in a maternal role, and as educators. Alfred's mother, in a well-known legend of the king's childhood, was shown assigning her sons a reading contest. Little Alfred sat by his mother's side, with other court ladies gathered protectively around him.[193]

Little space, then, in this world-view, for a woman who was neither a teacher nor a nurse, but instead distinguished herself as a ruler, town planner, diplomat and military leader. In all these capacities, Aethelflaed, if regarded at all, was perceived by the Victorians as standing firmly in her father's giant shadow.

The early nineteenth century did manage to name a few places after her, while softening her name to the more Latinate (and 'feminine') Ethelfleda. So Warwick has an Ethelfleda Mound – a hillock belonging, in fact, not to Aethelflaed's burh of Warwick, but to an early stage in construction of the Normans' castle in the town. (The name unfortunately gave rise to the mistaken notion that Aethelflaed 'built Warwick castle'.)

In 1823, fourteen years before the start of Victoria's reign, an article in the *Gentleman's Magazine* alluded to the burh at Tamworth as 'Ethelfleda's Tower'. The anonymous author is otherwise a little confused about Aethelflaed's identity. He recognises that she fortified Stafford, 'built in 913 by Ethelfleda, a Countess of Mercia'. He goes on to describe Wednesbury as built by one 'Adelfleda' – seemingly in his eyes a different person. He does, however, identify the said Adelfleda as 'Governess of the Mercian kingdom'.[194]

In 1863, while digging the foundations for a new bridge to carry the Widnes to Runcorn railway over the River Mersey, workmen came across evidence of earlier workings on the Runcorn site, dating from the tenth century. They could hardly be anything other than part of Aethelflaed's burh, built in 915 to keep watch over the Mersey Narrows. An application was made to the London and North Western Railway company to suspend work on their bridge, so that the site could be properly excavated. The railway project was already far behind schedule, however, and the company refused.[195]

By way of a belated apology, the LNWR named their new structure the Ethelfleda Bridge. Its pillars, in a mock castle design by the company's chief engineer William Baker, were a reference to the foundations of Aethelflaed's burh, now buried again beyond hope of retrieval beneath one of these very towers. Would the railway company have agreed to suspend construction of their bridge if the historic remains had been connected not with Aethelflaed, but with Alfred the Great? We shall never know.

The early twentieth century saw a revival of interest in Aethelflaed, largely focused around the anniversaries of towns she founded in the Midlands. These millennial events brought the figure of the Lady of the

Mercians into the foreground for the first time since the Middle Ages. Nationalistic sentiment, pride in the British Empire, and the earlier success of the Alfred millenary of 901, had much to do with the revival, as well as the resurgence of feminist ideals around women's fight to gain the vote. Women campaigning for their political emancipation could hardly fail to respect the Anglo-Saxon princess who had so effectively demonstrated the ability of a woman to rule a kingdom and to engage in the political life of her time. Civic pride in Aethelflaed as the founder of their towns seems, however, to have been the main motivator in citizens' bids to organise commemorative events.

Several towns presented pageants or similar outdoor spectacles, to celebrate their 'millenaries'. The pioneer in such projects was Warwick.[196] Although the burh there was not founded until 914, the Warwick council in 1906 invited the well-known American impresario Louis N. Parker to organise a pageant, on the strength of his success with an earlier historical event at Sherborne in Dorset. The Warwick citizens proposed, as their souvenir brochure for the event describes it, a commemoration of 'the thousandth anniversary of the Conquest of Mercia by Queen Ethelfleda'. If the historical concept was a little vague, the pageant remained a splendid event, with 2,000 actors, all of them local amateurs taking part, and seating for 4,800 spectators. It ran for six days, from 2 to 7 July, and covered not only a scene in which the Lady of the Mercians pardons captured Vikings and converts them to Christianity, but the arrival in Britain of the Romans, scenes involving Shakespeare and Queen Elizabeth I, and incidents from Warwickshire folklore. Much of the preparatory work for the pageant took place at a building on Jury Street in Warwick, which is known as Pageant House to this day.

Warwick might well have built upon the success of their 1906 event with a 1914 commemoration of the actual founding of the town a thousand years earlier, but the outbreak of the First World War intervened. The Warwick burh and its founder would have to wait another hundred years to be remembered at its proper time.

After Warwick, it was the turn of Stafford and Tamworth to celebrate the thousandth anniversary of their founding. Stafford in 1913 opted for a pageant organised by Martin Mitchell, with a script by C. S. Burne. In it, the Lady of the Mercians rode on horseback through admiring crowds. After ordered the founding of Stafford, she brought together Saxons and Danes, urging them to live together in harmony. 'Aethelfleda' then received the first Stafford Knot, the symbol of Stafford, as 'the bond that binds the five Hundreds of the town'.

The executive committee organising the town's pageant was chaired by Stafford's mayor, and numbered the Duke of Sutherland among its patrons. Special trains with cut-price fares brought visitors from as many as 125 miles away. An audience of 22,000 is said to have attended, even though the town's population was then only 26,000 – an indication of the pageant's widespread popularity, not only in Stafford itself, but across central England. Staged in the fields beside the ruins of Stafford castle, it saw five performances between 30 July and 4 August.[197]

The Bishop of nearby Lichfield gave an address, full of patriotic sentiment, part of which was quoted in the *Lichfield Mercury*:

> *One hopes that by such a vivid representation of Stafford's history ... we shall be stimulated to do our part in the great work of the present, and be filled with greater hope for the future, because it has been well said that the study of history is the best cordial for drooping spirits. And I hope that this pageant will stimulate your local patriotism and in turn your loyalty to your country.*

The local press has recorded the pageant's Aethelflaed section for posterity, with a photograph of Miss Nora Knight in the role of Aethelflaed. Miss Knight is a chubby-faced lady, mounted on a placid-looking white pony. Over her snowy-white wimple she has an elaborate, if anachronistic, crown, of a type worn by monarchs of the late Middle Ages. She and her horse are both draped in a voluminous train that would surely be a dangerous encumbrance on any battlefield. Her costume seems intended to denote Aethelflaed's regal status, rather than to represent her as a warrior. It is an image of the Lady of the Mercians as a founder, rather than a fighter.

Tamworth that year presented a play about Aethelflaed and her founding of the Tamworth burh, performed in the castle grounds on 9 and 10 July. As at Stafford, the focus in the Tamworth event was on Aethelflaed as a builder, rather than on her warrior role; her legacy presented as one that would endure through the centuries. Aethelflaed might have re-founded, expanded and fortified an ancestral Mercian palace after its destruction by Vikings rather than putting the name of Tamworth on the map for the very first time, but this was not going to keep local people from enjoying their Millenary. Early on the morning of 9 July, the bells of St Editha's were rung to announce the start of the event. There followed a mile-long procession through the town in which all the local schools took part, along with firemen and ambulance men, postal workers and a detachment of the Territorial Army. Two brass bands led the parade. Afterwards, a public luncheon was held at the Assembly Rooms. In the afternoon, before an audience packed with ladies in fashionable headgear and men in top hats and boaters, the Lady of the Mercians, played by Mrs Bessie Argyle, once again held court at Tamworth. Attended by ladies-in-waiting and guarded by her loyal thegns, she proclaimed the creation of the new burh. Something of the kind probably did take place in 913 – a discussion of the project with her witan, followed by a formal announcement of her intentions to her court, and to the town's inhabitants – no doubt fewer in number in 913. In 1913, 10,000 people are said to have attended the two-day millenary.[198]

Tamworth's event contributed something more lasting than amateur theatricals: Edward George Bramwell's statue of Aethelflaed, unveiled by the Earl and Countess Ferrers. Earl Ferrers spoke of Aethelflaed as a founder 'who knew how to inspire'. She was, he said, 'one of the best kind of foundresses … thinking not of herself, but of her country'. The people of Tamworth owed her 'a real debt'.

The Tamworth statue is probably the best-known representation of Aethelflaed anywhere. Bramwell's image of her is complex and somewhat ambivalent. His Lady of the Mercians is quite a matronly figure, clad in long 'womanly' robes. At the same time she holds, but does not brandish, a long sword, its point resting downwards at her feet. Her head, meanwhile, is turned sideways, to gaze down tenderly at her young nephew Athelstan, who returns her glance; while seeming about to draw the small dagger at his belt. (Offering, in his childish way, to defend his aunt? To defend Mercia against the Vikings?)

The whole scene is at once martial and maternal – Aethelflaed as warrior and nurturer both. It might have been expected that Aethelflaed's daughter Aelfwynn would be the object of the Lady's affectionate gaze. Aelfwynn, however, has here been erased from the historical record – much as her uncle Edward erased her from the political scene in her lifetime. She is supplanted by the male figure who would, after his aunt's death, unite the kingdoms of England under his rule.

The image is, ultimately, one of a female guardian who safeguards patriarchal power.

The inscription on the statue's base, however, contains no such ambiguity. It reads simply, 'To commemorate the Building of the Castle Mound by Aethelfleda the Lady of the Mercians', flanked by the dates 913 and 1913. We return to Aethelflaed as founder of the burh at Tamworth.

After the First World War, for one artist at least, the warrior image was remembered, and not favourably. Richard Caton Woodville (1865-1927) was a celebrated military artist, who painted scenes of war informed by his personal experience of combat. His depictions of 'Aethelflaed attacking Wales', in the 1922 edition of *Hutchinson's Story of the British Nation*, are far from idealised. In Woodville's imagined battle scene of Brecon Mere, Aethelflaed leads a mounted charge against helplessly overwhelmed Welsh foot soldiers. Scarcely able to defend themselves, they endure trampling under her horse's hooves, and cringe in terror at its feet. Woodville then depicts the victorious Aethelflaed after the battle, confronting a family group: the captured Welsh queen with her children. The Lady of the Mercians points away imperiously to her right – the queen and her offspring are to be taken as hostages. The children's faces register alarm and fright.

Behind the huddled women and children, and the men with spears who surround them, we see flames and the wreckage of war-ravaged buildings. Woodville's are images of the ugly face of war, in which the defeated expect no mercy. (In fact the Welsh queen and the other high-status prisoners were most probably well treated, and eventually ransomed. Her unfortunate subjects would have suffered much worse.)[199]

The northern Midlands in the twentieth and twenty-first centuries remain the part of England where the story of Aethelflaed and her achievements are most told and valued, and primarily for her work in building the region's towns. Wednesbury in Staffordshire, for instance, is the one place in England, other than Tamworth, to have a street named for Aethelflaed. Ethelfleda Terrace is an unpretentious strip of suburban road that runs along one side of a park, and up to St Bartholomew's churchyard, a quarter of a mile from the local Morrisons supermarket.

The ornamental gateway by the Wednesbury bus station known as the Caryatid Gate incorporates an image of Aethelflaed. The stylised work, designed by contemporary sculptor Steve Field, offers a striking contrast to the expressive humanity of the realistic statue in Tamworth. Here, the founder of Wednesbury's fortress clutches a sword, but hardly seems about to use it. She stares blank-faced with sightless eyes, as if in a trance – in some clairvoyant vision, perhaps, of what her fortified towns will one day become. For all its impersonality, this Aethelflaed is a commanding figure; not of a fighter, but of a leader and ruler of men, and a builder. We are back with the long view of Aethelflaed, as founder of the towns of the Midlands.

The slender bronze statue in the courtyard at Leicester Guildhall, with its robes, sceptre and crown, and the dignified expression on the finely modelled face, conveys a similar image. The sculpture of 'Ethelfloeda', as she is named on the plinth, is a replica of an original, made in 1922, that once adorned a drinking fountain in Victoria Park. The work of Benjamin Fletcher (1868-1951), a leading figure in the Arts and Crafts movement, the sculpture's basic conception came originally from the philanthropist who left £500 in her will to make it and donate it to the people of Leicester. Edith Gittins (1845-1910) was an artist, social reformer and active participant in the movement for women's suffrage; an outspoken advocate of education for women and of their right to take a full part in public life. One can well see why the figure of Aethelflaed would have appealed to her. Fletcher's statue, originally mounted on the drinking fountain, offers an ideal of a ruler who was also a public benefactor, dedicated to public service.

In 1978 the statue was stolen and replaced by a replica. After this copy was repeatedly vandalised, it was installed in a safer indoor space – eventually at the Guildhall. The inscription on a brass plaque behind the statue reads in part: 'Ethelfleda was the daughter of King Alfred the Great and as a leader of Mercia she repelled the Danes from Leicester in 918 A.D.' (Although she didn't actually 'repel' the Danish occupants, but rather took charge of the town, the point is taken.) Edith Gittins, too, is remembered here, as 'well known locally for her generous public service'. (Fletcher's name, curiously, is omitted; another artist, Jack Newport, is credited with the re-installation of the sculpture, in 1979.)

Tamworth has staged commemorations of its famous resident at regular intervals since the celebrated events of 1913. In 2013 its citizens, dressed in the fashions of a hundred years before, revisited the millenary to re-enact the unveiling of the Aethelflaed statue. May 2015 at Tamworth Castle saw an outdoor theatre performance of *Tigress*, a contemporary dance production narrating the story of Aethelflaed's defence of Mercia against the Vikings. Organised by the Motionhouse Dance Company, the production drew in a range of local talent – musicians, artists, craftspeople, community groups, and several dozen local schoolchildren.[200] The following year, the town added to its tributes to Aethelflaed, a decorated commemorative flagstone on the Ladybridge over the River Tame at its confluence with the Anker – one of a series recording the town's history.

Though it missed out on celebrating the millenary of 1914, Warwick, a hundred years later, would acknowledge Aethelflaed's role in the founding of their town by the erection of a small bronze plaque on a wall near the Castle Mound. The inscription on the plaque, surmounted by a stylised head and shoulders image of her, reads: 'Aethelflaed, Lady of the Mercians and daughter of Alfred the Great, founded a fortress at "Waeringwicum" in AD 914 which grew into the town of Warwick. Her conquest of the Viking "Danelaw" secured the creation of the Kingdom of England.'

Nothing could contrast more sharply with this modest image, than the hulking stone head that commemorates Aethelflaed's founding of the fortress at Runcorn. Now in the grounds of Runcorn's Brindley Theatre, Angela Sidwell's sculpture once stood overlooking the River Mersey, as if guarding against approaching invaders. Almost brutal in its stylised simplicity – a sphinx-like face on a roughly cut plinth, its broad features are impassively calm. Here there are no draperies, no sword, and a bowl-like cap or helmet in place of a crown or veil. The sculpture's very understatement compels attention. Stripped of all historical reference, it appears less as an attempted portrayal of a once-living person than as an evocation – of vigilance and of the will to endure. This Aethelflaed is an elemental figure, guardian genius of place.

Runcorn has two more images of Aethelflaed. There is one in wrought iron on a fence along the waterfront, close to the Ethelfleda Bridge, and the silver arch of the Jubilee road bridge. If less impressive than Sidwell's brooding stone head, the smiling female face, painted in dark blue, and with a fish swimming past its chin, evokes similar associations of Aethelflaed with the Mersey.

The other, in Runcorn's Old Town Bloom Community Garden, appears as a detail on an enormous mural that covers the end wall of a house. This one is a wild flight of fancy. Here, Aethelflaed holds her sword aloft in her right hand. She points it forward, almost as if about to hurl it like a spear. Her left arm is stretched out, the palm of her hand held upward like that of a police officer stopping traffic – the traffic in question being a stylised Viking ship with a sail or shroud twirled around its mast. In the manner of an illuminated capital on a medieval manuscript, the image as a whole forms the initial letter 'R' of the word 'Runcorn'. In the background are sketched castle walls and a church, suggesting Aethelflaed's burh.

Three churches in the Midlands contain stained glass windows depicting Aethelflaed: Worcester and Chester cathedrals; and St Andrew's, in the Gloucestershire village of Churchdown, where Aethelflaed is said to have herself endowed a church.

The Worcester Cathedral window, designed by A. J. Davies, an early twentieth century artist whose work is mainly associated with the Bromsgrove Guild, presents us with a fairly standard 'holy' image of a warrior or a saint – an idealised crowned female with breastplate and sword. The face – young, almost boyish, is calm and blank. This Worcester Aethelflaed, clad in gorgeous drapery, carries her sword in the crook of her arm, rather as if she were cradling a large bunch of flowers. The sword point is coyly concealed, tucked into the folds of her robe. The representation is clearly one of a warrior, but one may detect a certain ambivalence about the subject's connections with violence.

A copy of this image appears on a bronze plaque in Castle Street, Warwick, installed in 2014 to mark the 1100th anniversary of Aethelflaed's founding of the town.

The stained glass window in Churchdown, designed in 1934 by George Cooper-Abbs as one of a series depicting legendary local figures, is more clearly individualised. This Aethelflaed, done in green and gold, has long abundant tresses suggestive of some rural corn goddess. She looks stern and purposeful, unprepared to put up with any nonsense – Aethelflaed as Head Girl. Where the Worcester image has her holding a sword, the Churchdown figure wields a staff of office, or sceptre. The letter 'A' by her left shoulder surmounted by a crown, while alluding to her own name, could equally be an oblique tribute to Alfred, her father. The book to her right suggests her family's love of learning, and her own well-known piety. In another reminder of the culture that formed her, the patterning on her cloak echoes the traditional interwoven tracery of Anglo-Saxon metalwork and manuscript decoration. It is an attractive, if idealised, representation, evoking Aethelflaed's various roles as ruler, founder of churches, and patron of faith.

In Chester cathedral, the West Window, designed by W. T. Carter Shapland in 1961, depicts the Holy Family, flanked by six other images. Most are Saxons associated with the Midlands: Werburgh,

Oswald, Aidan, Chad and Wilfrid. Aethelflaed is the only non-saint in the row of eight tall standing figures that glow out at the viewer from the window's Perpendicular Gothic. As in the representation at Churchdown, she holds a sceptre, not a sword. Her place in this holy company is earned not by her military prowess, but by her reputation as a benign ruler who brought prosperity to her people.

Somewhat surprisingly for a figure known about mainly in a few corners of the Midlands, Aethelflaed has quite a substantial presence on the Internet. Much of it is expressed in the form of poster designs and other visuals – sometimes for the purpose of advertising. In the absence of any contemporary representation of her, twenty-first century artists, as much as their counterparts in the Middle Ages, have free rein for their imaginations. In these latter-day online conceptions of the Lady of the Mercians – unlike the twentieth-century ones in the towns and cathedrals – the focus is very much on her prowess as a female warrior.

One exception to this rule is a compelling head-and-shoulders image by Anna Fenn, on an educational website for the E2BN company, 'History's Heroes'. Fenn gives us a grey-eyed, serious Aethelflaed, simply clad in a dark red cloak and a dark veil. She gazes thoughtfully out at the world, as if contemplating the challenges ahead of her.[201]

Some of the Internet illustrations clearly aim to give a historically faithful picture of how Aethelflaed might have looked, dressed and behaved in battle. One of these realistic depictions has a caption under it: 'Aethelflaed, Lady of the Mercians, leads her Saxon warriors against the Danish Vikings at Derby, central England, 917 AD.' The illustration, by an anonymous artist, shows her mounted astride a rearing charger, wearing a helmet, and a cloak over a long dress. Her sword arm is flung back to strike the head of a Viking warrior. The Viking, in turn, is about to dispatch one of her thegns, who is tumbling backwards helplessly off the burh wall. The Viking looks likely to topple down on top of his victim, making Aethelflaed's rescue effort unnecessary. Still, it all makes for a dramatic technicolour scene.[202]

A more sober version of a helmeted Aethelflaed, 'in a series titled 'Women War Queens' from 'Deviantart', is proposed as 'A Quick

Concept Drawing for Aethelflaed'. This one, by the Australian artist Gambargin, has her ready for battle, on foot, standing proudly at the head of her troops. There is a fierce glint in her eyes – all that can be seen of her face behind the helmet, and her mask of chain mail. As if to assert her femininity within this traditionally masculine warlike role, foamy billows of blond hair, or possibly a veil, trickle down the sides of her head behind the mask. In addition to the helmet and mask she wears a full coat of chain mail, and her sword arm is protected by a mailed glove. Over the ranks of soldiers fly blue and yellow flags of Mercia – not, in fact, in existence in Aethelflaed's day, but a much later invention of antiquarians keen to put Anglo-Saxon Mercia back on the map.[203]

Despite the one minor anachronism, this is a clear attempt to come as close as possible to historical accuracy in representing the Lady of the Mercians on the brink of battle. It is a good deal more credible than, for instance, the recent depiction of Aethelflaed at Derby, in Stephen Pollington's otherwise excellent guide to the history of Anglo-Saxon Tamworth. Here, David Hobbs's illustration has her marching victorious onto the bloody battlefield wearing several layers of long clothing, but with nothing on her head but a light veil, 'dressed as if for a pleasant day's riding in the woods'. The historical Aethelflaed would surely have had the sense to wear a helmet?[204]

Some Internet representations of Aethelflaed, while retaining the warrior motif, veer wildly away from realism. One such image, by 'Chibi Sketches' (Marie Black), in a series titled 'Cool Chicks from History', portrays a visibly excited Aethelflaed, her mouth open in a war cry. She wears a sort of crinoline, while brandishing a spear in one hand and a sword in the other. She looks less like a Saxon warrior, than a Victorian housewife repelling a burglar by threatening him with the fire tongs. In this instance, the artist herself is clearly aware of the absurdity: 'Honestly, no,' she writes, 'she probably didn't wear that cloak or her crown into battle, but it makes a cool image, non?'[205]

Others posting their visions of the Lady of the Mercians show less sense of irony. 'Aethelflaed' by 'Edriss' (Jacqui Davis), for example, represents Aethelflaed as a dreamy-looking female in a long white gown, set against a pale wintry-looking background. For reasons not immediately apparent, she is seated side-saddle on the back of a brown bear. With a visionary expression, this Aethelflaed gazes into the far distance. She wears a helmet, but has another sitting at her feet. (A spare for emergencies?) Next to the helmet, propped awkwardly against the bear's chin, is what may be a sword – but looks more like a slender cricket bat. The figure grasps the naked blade of a more recognisable sword in both hands as it rests across her lap, in a way likely to do serious damage to her fingers. A round shield emblazoned with the dragon of Wessex is propped against the bear's behind. Wherever we are in this scene – the *Morte d'Arthur*, perhaps, or Fairyland – we are surely no longer in Mercia.[206]

Several other depictions, allegedly of the Lady of the Mercians, equally have little or nothing in common with the historical Aethelflaed except the name. Lupi McGinty has a small bowed gnome-like figure, suggestive of the world of Tolkien's *The Hobbit*.[207] 'Tigertwins' pictures Aethelflaed as a Disney-style princess, in a dress of what looks like blue denim, whose scared expression suggests that she expects to be ambushed.[208] 'Marasop', gives us a cute doll figure with exaggeratedly large blue eyes and plucked eyebrows.[209] Weirdest of all, perhaps, is a full-length poster image by an anonymous artist of a female warrior with tattooed arms and one bare breast prominently displayed. Against a background of dark skies, rocks and skulls, this figure looks out from the picture's frame with a hard sexual stare.[210] One can only wonder if Aethelflaed, who lived in a time when respectable women covered their bodies from neck to ankle, and often their heads as well, would have been offended, amused or simply astonished at this representation of her?

The Lady of the Mercians, in this internet world, is sometimes appropriated for the uses of commerce. If not a household name, she can still, it seems, be a brand name. Aethelflaed T-shirts, Aethelflaed beer – even Aethelflaed eye make-up – have from time to time been available online, nearly always with the main emphasis on Aethelflaed the female warrior.

In 2013, Aromaleigh cosmetics offered an Aethelflaed eye shadow for sale online as part of a series of makeup products called 'Ignis Antiquita' (Ancient Fire), 'inspired by history's forgotten women'.[211]

Aethelflaed has been marketed as a model figure for medieval war games. John Morris, who specialises in 'character sculpts' offers a pack of 'two 28mm scale miniature Aethelflaeds', 'unpainted, some assembly may be required'. One is a figure in a 'classical' pose, as 'we know her from art and statues', the other, a 'fighter' model, 'more practically equipped for the battlefield'. This second version 'COMES WITH A SHIELD!' Price: £8.00.[212]

The Sacre Brew company ('Wicked Artisanal Beers'), once had an attractive beer mat produced to advertise their Aethelflaed ale: 'An unhopped dark gruit ale made with herbs, much like what would have been brewed in the 10th century'. The advertisers' enthusiasm for Aethelflaed the warrior was unabashed. Without the Lady of the Mercians, they claimed, 'we'd all be speaking Danish in the Midlands. She definitively [sic] kicked Viking butt at the battle of Tettenhall'. José Carmona's design for the Aethelflaed ad depicts the head and shoulders of a dark-haired woman warrior, with fiercely sparkling light-coloured eyes. She wears late medieval war gear – pointed shield and metal breastplate, mailed gauntlets – suggesting, perhaps, Aethelflaed's kinship with a later heroine, Joan of Arc. (Now under new ownership, the company sadly no longer produces Aethelflaed Ale.)[213]

A number of novelists have been interested in representing Aethelflaed as a fictional character. At least seven novels about her appeared in the late 1990s and the 2000s. Haley Garwood's *Swords Across the Thames* (1999) was one of the first of these; followed by Rebecca Tingle's *The Edge on the Sword* (2001), Marjory Grieser's *King Alfred's Daughter* (2009), and Penny Ingham's *The King's Daughter* (2010). *To Be a Queen*, by Annie Whitehead, appeared in 2014. In all these fictions, Aethelflaed is the main character, the story narrated from her point of view.[214]

The character of Aethelflaed also features prominently in Bernard Cornwell's series of novels set in the time of King Alfred – notably in *Sword Song* (2007); *The Empty Throne* (2009); *The Burning Land* (2014); *Warriors of the Storm* (2015) and *The Flame Bearers* (2016), the most recent of Cornwell's 'Anglo-Saxon Stories'.[215]

In nearly all these fictions, the question of Aethelflaed's relationship with her husband is central. Garwood and Whitehead both present a loving relationship between Aethelflaed and Aethelred (although in *To Be a Queen* the love develops only slowly, out of initial coldness). In *The King's Daughter*, on the other hand, Aethelflaed feels nothing but revulsion for the man she has to marry, who is portrayed as insensitive and violent. Bernard Cornwell's Aethelred is an equally unpleasant character – vain, egotistical and ambitious, an incompetent leader, and coldly manipulative. There is no love lost between Aethelflaed and her husband, who resents his wife because she represents his dependency on his overlord King Alfred. He schemes to have another man force himself on Aethelflaed, so that he, Aethelred, will have grounds to divorce his wife for adultery. (In a note on his sources, Cornwell cheerfully admits that the story is his own invention, and that in fact he has been 'mightily unfair' to Aethelred: 'There is not a scrap of evidence', he concedes, that Aethelflaed's husband was as 'small-minded and ineffective as I make him out to be.'[216])

Rebecca Tingle's young-adult novel *The Edge on the Sword* covers a single year in the life of an adolescent Aethelflaed, as she moves from the security of her father's court to a new life with Aethelred (spelled here as 'Ethelred'), encountering and overcoming danger on the way. Unlike Cornwell's Aethelred, Tingle's Ethelred is caring and kind, giving his bride encouragement to perform her daunting new role as a ruler's wife. Before she even arrives at Ethelred's residence in Mercia, 'Flaed' has taken part in military action, and killed a Danish leader in self-defence. As she walks beside her bridegroom through London streets, feeling shabby and inadequate for her role, she hears the people praising her courage, and knows she has found acceptance as the new Lady of the Mercians. In Tingle's version of the relationship with her husband, there is no attempt on his part to undermine her courage or suppress her independence.[217]

All seven novelists bend historical fact outrageously, in the interests of building more dramatic stories. Anyone relying on these fictions to reconstruct an accurate biography of Aethelflaed would come away with some odd ideas indeed.

The novels intended for adult readers all manage to incorporate some kind of love triangle involving Aethelflaed – often involving the Vikings. In *Swords Across the Thames*, for instance, Eiric the Dane yearns hopelessly after the Mercian princess. The Aethelflaed of *The King's Daughter* has (most improbably), a love affair with King Alfred's old adversary and baptised convert, Guthrum. 'May Frig, the goddess of love forgive him', reflects the Dane, 'he had fallen in love with her'. Aethelflaed even bears a son to Guthrum, although the child does not survive long enough for anyone else to discover the fact.[218]

In *To Be a Queen*, while remaining sexually faithful to Aethelred, Aethelflaed still pines for the man she would have preferred to marry, and flirts with a Welsh chieftain by way of compensation. Bernard Cornwell's heroine – who has also had a Viking lover in her youth – falls in love with Uhtred, narrator of the Saxon Stories, who has been told in a prophecy that he would win the love of 'a creature of gold'.[219]

The fictional Lady of the Mercians gets captured and kidnapped a few times – something that, as far as we know, never happened to the historical Aethelflaed. Travelling to her new married life in Mercia, the Aethelflaed of *To Be a Queen* has a narrow escape from a Viking ambush.[220] Cornwell's Aethelflaed is first captured by Danes (*Sword Song*), having to be rescued by Uhtred; then, in *The Burning Land*, is besieged in a convent by the unpleasant Aldhelm, whom Aethelred has sent to force his wife into adultery. (Again, it is Uhtred who rides to the rescue.) Penny Ingham's character in *The King's Daughter* even narrowly escapes being burned alive as a sacrifice to the pagan gods. It's a wonder she had any time left for building burhs or fighting Vikings.

In two of the novels where she appears, the representation of Aethelflaed's daughter Aelfwynn is also controversial. As portrayed in both *Swords Across the Thames* and *To Be a Queen*, Aelfwynn is the archetypal stroppy teenager. She sulks, throws tantrums, and accuses her mother of neglecting her in favour of ruling Mercia. In *To Be A Queen* Aelfwynn has sex with the thegns of Aethelflaed's court, in a bid to punish her mother. After Aethelflaed's death, her only interest is in taking possession of her mother's clothes. This Aelfwynn is never allowed to become the second lady of the Mercians. By general agreement of Aethelflaed's followers, 'She would have us eating Viking herring within a month.'[221] Haley Garwood takes the motif even further, having Aethelflaed on her deathbed actually disinherit Aelfwynn. Aethelflaed then demands that her history be erased from the *Anglo-Saxon Chronicles*: 'I do not want Wyn to have any claim to the Mercian throne because of my conquests. Take my name out of history.'[222]

Of the historical novelists who have represented the Lady of the Mercians in their work, Cornwell is the most successful. It helps, probably, that he makes no attempt to imagine the subjective world of any of the historical figures who people his Saxon Stories, preferring to represent them as seen through the eyes of his fictional main character, Uhtred. Cornwell's Aethelflaed, viewed by his hero, is a commanding presence – imperious to subordinates at times, but also capable of warmth and compassion; a free spirit, who has 'mischief and life and laughter'.[223] Cornwell's recently married Aethelflaed, still an adolescent, asserts herself early on, in support of a military mission to be undertaken by Uhtred:

> *None of you have the courage to fight alongside Uhtred?'*
> *Aethelflaed demanded of the watching men. She was*
> *fourteen years old, a slight, pale girl, yet in her voice*
> *was the lineage of ancient kings. 'My father would want*
> *you to show courage tonight!' she went on, 'or am I to*
> *return to Wintanceaster and tell my father that you sat by*
> *the fires while Uhtred fought?*[224]

Having rallied the troops to follow Uhtred, Aethelflaed then extracts an oath of loyalty from him. She was probably at least a year older when she married, than Cornwell represents her. But the fire and confidence he depicts are highly credible. Moreover, his fictional character is seen to develop over time. In Cornwell's conception, her personality is 'curdled' and embittered by her unhappy marriage.[225] The 40-year-old ruler of Mercia has 'a hard face', although 'men said she had been beautiful as a young woman'. In later life she has developed 'a gaze … that could unsettle the bravest of men … cold and thoughtful, as if she were reading your thoughts and despising them'. She 'seemed to dislike most people', we are told; and yet 'she was adored in Mercia'.[226]

While imagining a subjective life of thoughts and emotions for their character, most of the novelists are less successful at representing Aethelflaed in her public roles as queen in all but name. In spite of preposterous fictional inventions that give his narrator Uhtred credit for ninety per cent of what happens in ninth- and tenth-century England – including personally engineering the appointment of Aethelflaed as the Mercians' ruler after Aethelred's death – Cornwell thoroughly understands her world, and the roles she would have played in it. Unlike Whitehead's Aethelflaed and those of other recent novelists, Cornwell's character shows no urge to check the kitchen stores, inspect the bakery, order new table linen, plan the palace menu, or carry away buckets of mud to help in building a burh – all activities undertaken by other fictional Aethelflaeds. He knows there would have been servants, slaves and conscripted peasants performing such tasks.[227]

One particularly irritating feature of many of the 'Aethelflaed' novels is the perceived need to give the heroine, and sometimes supporting characters too, folksy nicknames. Aethelflaed is called Lae (*Swords Across the Thames*), Flaed (*The Edge on the Sword*); and most oddly of all, in *To Be a Queen*, Teasel. Garwood, along with 'Lae' for Aethelflaed, has a whole American-sounding family, in which Aethelred is referred to as 'Red'; Athelstan becomes 'Stan', and one of the Vikings' young sons is referred to as 'Kerby'. Only Ingham and Cornwell refrain from insulting their readers' intelligence in this way: Ingham has 'Elflaede', while Cornwell consistently calls Aethelflaed by her proper name.

A mention should be made here of the portrayal of Aethelflaed on TV. It is, after all, an image that has made the legend of the Lady of the Mercians – if in an often sensational and inaccurate form – known to millions in Britain and the United States. In the recent BBC dramatisation of Cornwell's novels, as *The Last Kingdom*, Millie Brady gives a most convincing performance as the young Aethelflaed, suggesting in turn intelligence, courage, dignity and self-possession, and a zest for life.[228]

And what of the non-fictional biographers, and the academic historians? Have their conceptions of the Lady of the Mercians altered, since the time when F. T. Wainwright offered his groundbreaking essay calling for a new appreciation of this forgotten heroic figure from the Anglo-Saxon past? Wainwright emphasised Aethelflaed's willing cooperation with her younger brother – to the point where she was prepared to subordinate her own plans and fame to that of Edward.[229] Paul Hill and Stephanie Hollis have both, to varying degrees, questioned this view. Hollis in particular emphasises Aethelflaed's pursuit of policies that tended to make Mercia more independent of Wessex. This bid for independence is, I believe, a major factor in Edward's deposition of Aelfwynn as the second Lady of the Mercians, after her mother's death.[230]

Until recently, modern scholars have followed the lead of Aethelflaed's near-contemporary chroniclers, in focusing on her military role – her successes as a commander and strategist. So, for Hill, for instance, Aethelflaed was primarily a 'redoubtable' military figure, 'a leader who accompanied her army in the field and who certainly directed military operations from the saddle.'[231]

Though she titles her biography *The Warrior Queen*, and writes of Aethelflaed's military campaigns in some detail, Joanna Arman is at pains to emphasise that her subject was 'a well-rounded human being'. She acknowledges Aethelflaed's other skills, as a founder of burhs and a diplomat. Her book's main emphasis, though, is on the Lady of the Mercians as a fighter.[232]

Other historians have increasingly tended to view Aethelflaed from more diverse perspectives. While in most cases their attention to the Lady of the Mercians has been given only briefly, in the space of a few pages and the context of a larger encompassing project – still, they are more inclined to view this fascinating figure in the round – not only for her heroism and skilful military leadership in defending

Mercia against invaders, but for her abilities as a ruler, a diplomat, a builder of towns, and patron of the church.

For Tom Holland, Aethelflaed is simply the 'founding mother' of what, under Aethelstan, would become for the first time a united England – her achievement not only to win back Derby and Leicester from Viking rule, but to bring into being the safety, prosperity and stability upon which her nephew Athelstan would later build.[233]

Mary Dockray-Miller, clearly uneasy with Aethelflaed's military role within the inherited patriarchal social structures of Anglo-Saxon England, stresses her 'maternal' activities as a defender and protector of her kingdom and its inhabitants: 'Even at her most aggressive, her goals were the protection of her people and the reclamation of territory previously taken by the Vikings.' Dockray-Miller also stresses the success of Aethelflaed's building projects, and the skills they called for. Her burh building project was, she writes, 'a daunting task that required knowledge of materials, building techniques, worker management and military necessity. It shows Aethelflaed to be a perceptive and dedicated manager.'[234]

Don Stansbury, writing in 1993, had already made points similar to Dockray-Miller's. He argues that Aethelflaed brought 'the influence of a woman' to the government of Mercia: 'Her rule had been fair and intelligent. It was a healing, harmonious way.' Stansbury gives a somewhat idealised account of Aethelflaed's achievements, however – seeking to distinguish her exercise of power and resort to military force from that of her male counterparts, notably the Viking leaders, and of her brother Edward. She is for Stansbury the *Lady* who fought the Vikings – and that, he contends, makes all the difference. She engaged in warfare only when necessary, he argues, and not for conquest, but to create peace and prosperity for her society as a whole. Her feminine influence is emphasised as a means of countering masculine proneness to violence – what Stansbury terms, the 'Viking way'. Aethelflaed's, by contrast, was 'the woman's' way: 'The dangerous world that she had been born into, the world that men had dominated and made dangerous, could be civilised, made prosperous and safe by a woman and perhaps only by a woman.'[235]

Tellingly, Stansbury's account of Aethelflaed's career omits the story of the savage punitive raid on Llangorse / Brecon Mere, and the destruction of the settlement there. Her work in founding towns, on the other hand, is almost lovingly described. And when he argues that Aethelflaed did not regard fighting as 'a sport' – evidently a view held by Danes and Norsemen, and probably quite a few Anglo-Saxons too – but as an occasional unpleasant necessity, he may well have a point.[236] Stansbury does not, however, share Dockray-Miller's reservations about the value of a woman participating in, and by implication supporting, the patriarchal social order.

Victoria Thompson is interested in Aethelflaed's work as a patron of religious buildings, and in what they meant to her and her culture in terms of both piety and prestige. She points out that while she might have been 'unusual as a ruler', Aethelflaed was in many respects 'representative of her class and gender, as aristocratic daughter, sister, wife and mother' – not least in her founding of shrines and churches. While her position enabled her to endow religious sites on a grand scale, Aethelflaed's activities were otherwise typical of high-status Anglo-Saxons in the early tenth century.[237]

Recent historians do well to offer such shifts of emphasis from Aethelflaed's undoubted heroism in battle – without which her kingdom would not have survived – onto a broader picture of her contributions to her world as a whole. The names of her battles are, today, known mainly to historians. The sites of churches she endowed, built, restored, even if the original buildings have mostly vanished and the church's names have changed – remain. The towns she founded and fortified mapped out the shape of the English Midlands. For those who care to notice it, the evidence of her work is everywhere – in Worcester, in Oxford, in Gloucester, Tamworth, Stafford, Warwick, Derby. In Runcorn, Bridgnorth, Shrewsbury ...

'If you seek a monument – look around.'

Where to Find Her

Bridgnorth

The locals insist on dating their town from a mere 900 years ago –
from 1101, to be precise, when a Norman lord built a castle here. In
fact the town goes back nearly another 200 years. With the hilltop and
the river together forming a natural defence system, and a sweeping
view over open country to the east, this is one of the best strategic
locations on the west bank of the Severn. It is almost certainly the
place referred to in the *Anglo-Saxon Chronicles* where Aethelflaed
built a burh in 912. A pretty market town (population 12,000), with
its castle, its museum, and a handsome eighteenth-century gatehouse
at Northgate, Bridgnorth has won an award for its High Street, and is
all-over historic.

Street plan
Bridgnorth was newly laid out in the twelfth century – re-founded,
in effect – and the layout of its main streets probably changed
somewhat at that point. The shape of the town was further altered
by a devastating fire caused by an explosion in St Leonard's church
during the English Civil War that burned down a wide area to the
northeast.

There isn't much of a grid layout in the upper part of Bridgnorth,
known as High Town, where the streets snake across the hill in all
directions. Still, we might wonder if the central highways of a Saxon
burh once crossed one another at right angles where the present
Westgate Street meets the High Street. (Westgate becomes Church
Street on the other side of the crossroads.)

The church

The most likely spot for the original burh church, is where St Leonard's stands today. Rebuilt in the seventeenth century, and again in the nineteenth, the building is said to have fragments of Saxon stone incorporated in its walls.[238]

The church is sited on the very highest point of the hill. Apart from the spiritual protection the townspeople would hope for from their church, a lookout posted here could spot an approaching attacker from miles away, and sound the alarm.

The burh wall may have run round the hill's base, along the Severn's western bank, and there may have been Saxon settlement at some point in Bridgnorth's Low Town, with its easy access to the river. But the logical place for the centre of Aethelflaed's burh is High Town, right up on top of the hill.

Chester

The oblong, 800yds by 400, that forms Chester's 'Aethelflaedan' burh, takes its shape from the boundary formed by the town's surviving Roman walls. The burh's main streets are also Roman in origin. Eastgate and Watergate streets, intersected by Northgate Street and Bridge Street, today have their central crossroads marked marked by a stone column, the Chester Cross.

The Church

Now the Cathedral Church of Christ and the Blessed Virgin Mary, this is where Aethelflaed brought the relics of St Werburgh for safety, and established a second shrine to St Oswald. The original church, once dedicated to St Werburgh (which became a Benedictine abbey), has long since disappeared. (The cathedral guides will tell you, however, that the saint's remains may have survived the wholesale destruction of relics at the time of Henry VIII's Reformation; that they may still be buried somewhere on the cathedral premises.) An imposing shrine to St Werburgh, erected in the nineteenth century upon the original medieval base, stands in the cathedral's Lady Chapel.

Stained glass

The beautiful twentieth-century stained glass image of Aethelflaed ('Ethelfleda') by W. T. Carter Shapland, can be seen in the cathedral's West Window, in the company of the Holy Family, with St Werburgh, St Oswald, and others Aethelflaed venerated in her lifetime.

City Walls

Many times restored since Aethelflaed rebuilt the Roman originals, Chester walls are known as a tourist attraction in themselves. Lower parts of the walls, and whole sections of them to the north of the city, show traces of their original Roman construction. It is possible to walk the entire circumference of the existing town centre on the fairly broad pavement that now runs between the parapets above the streets.

While much of the history associated with the walls relates to the later Middle Ages, or to the English Civil War, a memory of the Lady of the Mercians lingers in the legend of Bonewaldesthorne's Tower – otherwise known as the Water Tower – a medieval structure at the walls' north-western corner. The tower is said to be named after an officer in Aethelflaed's army.

Churchdown

A village in Gloucestershire, between Gloucester and Cheltenham, where Aethelflaed is said to have owned land and founded a church. If she did build one here, its location is unknown.

Stained glass

The small but lovely green-and-gold stained glass window of 1934, designed by George Cooper-Abbs and installed in the existing church of St Andrew, is a fitting tribute to Aethelflaed.

Church opening times

The church is often open between services, and there are helpful and friendly staff. They have a website that gives information on opening times: www.standrewschurchdown.org.uk

Gloucester

The town retains some of the most interesting and moving traces of Aethelflaed's work for Mercia.

Market cross

Laid out to the four points of the compass. You can walk along Westgate Street and the other streets where Aethelflaed walked and rode. Longsmith Street, where the metalworking trades developed; St Aldate Street, the cattle market street called the Oxebode, are all still in existence, their names unchanged from Saxon times. After 1,100 years, although its main location has shifted to King's Square, a central market still does business at the Market Cross every Friday. St Michael's Tower at the Cross, all that remains of a fifteenth-century church, is said to be built on the site of a Saxon church.

The Tower, now the HQ of Gloucester Civic Trust, is staffed by dedicated and friendly volunteers, and open to the public. The staff host films, talks and history walks in Gloucester, plus tea and cake for a very modest sum. Phone 01452 526955 for opening hours.

Church

Keep walking westward from Gloucester Cathedral, at the western end of the city, and you come to the ruined wall of St Oswald's Priory. Though much restored, a small part of the masonry dates from Aethelflaed's time. It's an atmospheric place – especially if you reflect that this was an important religious shrine, attracting pilgrims from all over England, and that two rulers of Mercia were buried here.

Graves

Although an estimated seven generations of Saxons were laid to rest in graves around the exterior of St Oswald's, and some of their skeletons were found during excavation of the site in the 1970s, no one any longer knows exactly what became of the remains of Aethelflaed and her husband. They were almost certainly interred in the free-standing crypt at the church's east end. In the 1970s attempts were made to excavate the crypt, covered by grass and outbuildings in the back gardens of two houses along St Mary's Street. These efforts were brought to a halt after only a quarter of the space had been dug out, due to the danger of working in the treacherously sliding sand which had filled the crypt. Even by then, it was clear the mausoleum had been thoroughly plundered – presumably by thieves, rather than by the zealots of the Reformation.

The city museum has on display an ornately carved stone slab found during excavations at St Oswald's, that may once have covered a royal grave.

Sculpture

Although nothing has as yet been finalised, there are plans to put up a statue to Aethelflaed in Gloucester, in 2018.

Palace

Excavations at Kingsholm in the 1970s focused on Deanery Road and on Kingsholm Square, a few yards from Gloucester's rugby ground. Among other finds, the archaeologists uncovered evidence of a late-Saxon timber building, thought to be the royal residence in Gloucester where Aethelred and Aethelflaed once held court, and where Edward the Confessor and William the Conqueror presided over their councils, in their turn.[239]

Foundations and post holes at the site suggested a bow-sided building, that widened on either side towards the middle of its length, rather like the sides of a boat. 'If their late Saxon date is not in question,' the archaeologists concluded cautiously, 'the most natural interpretation of the documentary evidence' was that this was the site of Aethelred and Aethelflaed's palace.

The timber-built hall was about half a mile from the town wall, and within easy walking distance of both the town and St Oswald's. If you follow Dean's Walk from St Oswald's Priory to Kingsholm, you are walking the original 1,100-year-old track that ran from St Oswald's church to the palace.

Hereford

Burh wall

The town has the distinction of containing the only surviving remnants of original Saxon burh defences from the 900s. The first phase of these had a drystone wall, part of which is still intact, with a timber palisade. The contemporary reconstruction of the oak palisade atop the wall seems surprisingly low to function as an obstacle to armed warriors, and the vertical posts set into it, quite slender. The fence posts of the palisade at Tamworth, by contrast, were fashioned of whole tree trunks, stout enough to repel hordes of Vikings. A fairly determined burglar could get over the palisade reconstruction at Hereford, let alone a Viking army. However that may be, the original stones that formed the base of the burh wall can be seen at the rear of St Owen's Court, near the junction of St Owen's and Cantilupe Street. The wall continues along the back of a row of houses on Mill Street, to the garden of number 19, Cantilupe.[240]

Leicester

Sculpture

Benjamin Fletcher's small, elegant statue of Aethelflaed at the Leicester Guildhall owes its existence to the generosity of the artist, philanthropist and ardent feminist, Edith Gittins. A replica can be found in the Leicester Guildhall courtyard, mounted on a plinth that replaces the original drinking fountain.

Church

Aethelflaed left her mark on this Viking-occupied town, which surrendered to her in 918 without a fight. It is thought that St Mary de Castro, 'the premier church of late-Saxon Leicester' was either founded or rebuilt by Aethelflaed after she took the city.[241] The present church building is said to have been established in 1107; but this twelfth-century 'founding' seems in practice to have entailed the restoration of an earlier, 'collegiate' church that existed prior to the Norman conquest. After the building of Leicester Castle, the church fell within the castle precinct – hence its current name.

Oxford

Surprisingly for a town with an international reputation for early medieval scholarship, there is little visible evidence of the Lady of the Mercians here, even though Oxford was founded by Aethelred and Aethelflaed as a wholly new urban community. The pair deserve more conspicuous credit for their achievement. If Aethelflaed's father Alfred did not, as the Victorians liked to believe, establish Oxford University, his daughter and her husband did found the town. They made the city of dreaming spires possible.

The original street plan has changed little in over 1,100 years and the layout of Aethelred and Aethelflaed's burh is easy to trace when walking through the town centre. Castle Street and High Street run west to east, and are intersected by the north-south axis of Cornmarket/St Aldate's Street. A circular route around this basic cross – St Michael and Ship Streets, School Street and Oriel Street, once formed the inner 'ring road' that ran along the inside of the burh walls. St Aldate's church in the southwest of the town would have been safely enclosed within them.

Runcorn

Bridge

It's still possible to cross from Widnes to Runcorn on the Ethelfleda railway bridge over the Mersey, with its darkly impressive castellated towers, to the spot where the foundations of Aethelflaed's burh on the Runcorn side were briefly uncovered when building the bridge in 1863. It's a 30-minute journey, and local trains run from Widnes every half an hour. (Less frequently in the evenings.)

The bridge itself has been somewhat upstaged in recent years, by the gleaming arc of the Silver Jubilee road bridge, built parallel to the railway line. It may still be worth walking the short distance from the High Street to the attractive waterfront, to have a look at both bridges, and across the Mersey Narrows to Widnes on the other side.

Church

The many-times re-founded church on Church Street, now a Victorian building called All Saints, is traditionally said to have been established by Aethelflaed to serve and protect the new burh. Its earliest known dedication was to St Bertelin (Beorhthelm).

Sculpture and painting

Ten years ago, the powerful, enigmatic representation of Aethelflaed by Angela Sidwell, with its companion statues of an anonymous Saxon and a Viking, stood on Wigg Island, overlooking the Mersey. Designed by Sidwell, the sculptures were completed as a community project, with the participation of local schoolchildren who did some of the preparatory carving. They are now easily found by a visitor to Runcorn, at the front entrance to Runcorn's Brindley Theatre, on Leiria Way. (Between the High Street and the canal.)

Aethelflaed is remembered, too, on Runcorn's waterfront, with a representation of her as 'Aethelfreada' on the wrought-iron fence of a lookout point near the Jubilee Bridge. She also performs as a decorative capital on the 'R' of Runcorn, on a huge mural in the Old Town Bloom Community Garden. (Ask a local resident for directions.)

144

Shrewsbury

This site seems purpose-designed by nature for a fortress: cradled in a bend of the Severn that almost makes the town an island; perched on a hilltop with a far-reaching view over the Severn valley below. Apparently Aethelflaed thought so too. Shrewsbury's original name, 'Scrobbesbyrig', means 'fortified place in the scrubland'.

Though local tradition gives the town's founding date as 912, Shrewsbury is sometimes said to have been one of the earliest Mercian burhs to be built, along with Oxford, Hereford and Gloucester. It's possible that while the founding charter for the new burh was signed as early as 901, construction did not, for whatever reason, take place until much later. Shrewsbury is now the county town of Shropshire, with a population of approximately 100,000.[242]

Church
One of several hundred listed buildings in Shrewsbury, St Alkmund's, now partly medieval in construction, part eighteenth century, is unusual in having retained the name and dedication of the original 'Aethelflaedan' church. This is where Aethelflaed is said to have brought the remains of St Alkmund (Ealhmund) from Derby, to keep them safe from the Danes and to bless the newly established town. As at Bridgnorth, with which the site has much in common, the burh church stands on the highest point of the hill with a view in every direction. Apart from the spiritual protection the church and its holy relics were believed to confer, the building could have served as an effective watchtower and early warning system.

For opening hours to visitors at St Alkmund's, see the church's website: www.stalkmundschurch.co.uk

Stafford

The main street of Stafford runs from north to south. In the middle, it is called Greengate Street. At the northern end, where a town gate would once have stood, it changes its name to Gaolgate. At the burh's opposite end, this long main thoroughfare of Greengate changes its name a third time, to Bridge Street.

It used to be thought that Market Square, and another stretch of road – confusingly named, like the main street, Greengate – running from west to east across the main north-south thoroughfare, formed the original burh cross. However, Martin Carver, who in 2010 published a report on his excavations in the town, suggests the Saxon main streets may originally have formed roughly the perimeter of a rectangle around St Mary's church: travelling clockwise from Earl Street at the west of the rectangle, running along the top of it on Broad Street. This northern street would then have once connected to Greengate street, which in turn joins with Mill Street at the bottom. (A look at Google Maps for Stafford town centre makes this description a lot clearer.)[243]

Bridge
There is still a bridge on Bridge Street, as Greengate Street becomes at its end nearest the River Sow. The bridge leads over the Sow, and away from the town centre towards the suburbs. Once across the bridge you have left Aethelflaed's burh.

Church
The excavated site of St Bertelin's, thought to have been the original burh church, is close to where St Mary's collegiate church stands today. The St Bertelin site is easy to find: marked as Number 29 on the excellent map of Stafford provided by the Leisure Services department of Stafford Council, in connection with its Stafford heritage trail: http://www.staffordbc.gov.uk/live/Documents/Leisure%20Services/Stafford-Trail.pdf

Pageantry
Stafford is proud of its founding by Aethelflaed, and over the years has hosted occasional processions and pageants that commemorate the event – in 1913, and again in 2013. These are usually announced

in the Staffordshire Newsletter, and on the 'Enjoy Staffordshire' website: http://www.enjoystaffordshire.com/whats-on/

Tamworth

Sculpture
Tamworth is a place that proclaims, 'Aethelflaed was here'. The pleasant Staffordshire market town on the border with Warwickshire, with a river and a spacious park around its Norman castle, has the best-known image of Aethelflaed, the 1913 'millenary' statue by Edward George Bramwell. Also a decorative flagstone on the Ladybridge over the River Tame. A new twenty-foot statue, by Luke Perry, was erected in 2018, outside Tamworth railway station.

Pageantry
Tamworth is the Midlands town that has seen the most celebrations and commemorations of the Lady of the Mercians: a play and the unveiling of the statue in 1913; a re-enactment of the unveiling in 2013; a contemporary dance performance in 2015.

The burh
The site of the castle overlooking the convergence of the rivers Tame and Anker, is where the Saxon royal residence, ransacked and burned by Viking raiders, and built anew by Aethelflaed, once stood. The well-known statue in front of the Norman castle records Aethelflaed's founding of the burh. The castle museum, while it focuses on the post-Norman Conquest period, also contains information on Anglo-Saxon history.

The Tamworth burh main streets are Church Street and Lichfield Street, intersecting with Silver Street/Holloway. If we imagine an encircling outer wall around this central cross, with its either end running down to the riverside, it is possible to picture how Aethelflaed's burh as a whole would have looked when first built. The church on the far side of the main streets from the castle, and the site of the palace where the castle now stands, can then be viewed as elements in a single fortified complex.

Church

St Editha, to whom the church is now dedicated, was Aethelflaed's niece, Athelstan's sister. The church site almost certainly dates back to Aethelflaed's founding of the burh, but the saint to whom the church was originally dedicated, is unknown.

Warwick

Though the town has commemorated the Lady of the Mercians as its founder, in 1906 and again in 2014, there seems to be a good deal of confusion about her in Warwick. 'She built the Castle', residents will say. There is no information about Aethelflaed in the town's Market Hall Museum (although it does display a few exquisite pieces of Anglo-Saxon jewellery).

Burh layout

The commercial focus of the town has shifted away from the original main streets, possibly owing to the volume of traffic that flows through them, but the burh's main crossroad is easy to locate. Northgate, Church Street and Castle Street form a cross with the High Street and its continuation, Jury Street.

Gatehouse

The eastern limit of the Aethelflaedan burh is marked by an imposing gatehouse, originally built in the eleventh century, with eighteenth-century rooms above it.

Church

The burh church stood at the east of the market place, on a site now occupied by the magnificent medieval church of St Mary, with its ornate late-medieval and Tudor tombs of the Warwick family.

A climb up the 160 steps of the narrow, spiralling, tube-like church tower is definitely not for the faint-hearted. But it does reward the climber with a bird's-eye view of the town below. Looking down from this height gives a sense of how compact, how close to its original burh layout Warwick remains today. (The exception to this is to the south of the town, where the Norman castle took a large slice out of the burh on that side, and blocked direct access to the River Avon.)

Plaque
The plaque put up in 2014 to mark 1,100 years since Aethelflaed founded Warwick, is on the side wall of the Court House at the end of Jury Street, home of the Tourist Information Office. As you go out through the side door of the tourist office into Castle Street, the plaque is just to your left, by the entrance to the Pageant Garden.

Wednesbury

Sculpture
That Aethelflaed founded Wednesbury, is an article of faith with the town's local historians. Whether she did or not, Steve Field's contemporary representation of Aethelflaed keeps watch night and day at the Wednesfield bus station. With her veiled head, she holds up the left side of the Caryatid Gate, an archway topped with giant silver-coloured horns. Her partner in this work on the right-hand side is a representative of twenty-first century Wednesbury, a tube-maker in contemporary work clothes.

Ethelfleda Terrace
A suburban road at the side of a sloping park planted with ornamental trees, leads up from High Bullen, the A462, to the hilltop above. A street sign on the left at the top reads, 'Ethelfleda Terrace'.

Church

The present building, St Bartholomew's, dates from Tudor times, but the site's recorded history goes back to the eleventh century. Walking around the building's exterior – beware of slippery pavements in wet weather – it becomes clear that this spot at the summit of Church Hill would make an ideal defensive position. From here, you can still see for several miles to the north across open countryside. Before buildings obstructed the view, it would have been possible to see in all directions. An excellent lookout, this place would have been easy to defend against attack from below.

Worcester

The centre of Mercia's religious and cultural life for centuries, Worcester remained a key administrative centre, even after the rise in importance of the newly restored Gloucester. Worcester is known for the charters signed there by Aethelflaed and her husband, and the reinforcement of its burh, 'for the protection of all the people'.

Stained glass

A. J. Davies's idealised image of Aethelflaed as a warrior saint (minus the halo) can be seen in Worcester cathedral. It is the model for the representation of Aethelflaed on the 2014 commemorative plaque in Warwick.

Notes

1: A Wartime Childhood

1 'You have hurled us back.' Psalm 44, 10-11.

2 A theory suggested by Paul Hill in *The Viking Wars of Alfred the Great*. Barnsley, 2008, p.48.

3 surprise attack ... Chippenham. In *The Anglo-Saxon Chronicles*, (ASC), ed. and trans. M. Swanton, 2nd edn, London, 2001, p.75.

4 '... drowned in the sea.' Simeon of Durham, chronicle entry for 793, in *The Historical Works of Simeon of Durham*, ed. and trans. Stevenson, London, 1855. Quoted in G. Jones. *A History of the Vikings*, Oxford. 1984, p.196.

5 Alcuin's letter to Aethelred, king of Northumbria: http://historyonline.chadwyck.co.uk/getImage?productsuffix=_studyunits&action=printview&in=gif&out=pdf&src=/ehd/ehd00189/conv/ehd00189.pdf&IE=.pdf. Accessed in September 2017.

6 God's punishment: Jeremiah, 1:17.

7 'dreadful forewarnings': ASC for 793, pp. 55, 57.

8 An Irish chronicler. *Fragmentary Annals of Ireland*, (FA), ed. J. Radner. Dublin, 1978, p.169.

9 'Deliver us ... realms.' Quoted in Magnusson, *Vikings!* New York,1980, p.6.

10 'This I desire ...' Abbo of Fleury's 'Life of St. Edmund, King of East Anglia'. In Sweet, *Anglo-Saxon Primer*, 9th edn, trans. K. Cutler, Oxford, 1961, pp. 81-87.

11 Origin of the term, 'Viking'. Famous for ...'wics'. Alternative explanations for the term 'Viking' are that it refers to the Old Norse for a fjord, or that it is the name of a place in Scandinavia the invaders were believed to come from. A useful exploration of this question can be found in K. Holman, *The A to Z of the Vikings*, Lanham, Maryland, 2009.

12 making plans for the long term. ASC, p.64.

13 'annihilated to a man'. Asser, *Life of King Alfred*, ed. and trans. S.Keynes and M.Lapidge, in *Alfred the Great, Asser's* Life of King Alfred *and other contemporary sources*, London, 1983, p.81.

14 'struck out ... against the Vikings': ASC p.75; Asser, p.84.

15 William of Malmesbury and the legend of St Cuthbert: William of Malmesbury, *Chronicle of the Kings of England: From the earliest period to the reign of King Stephen*, ed. and trans. J.A. Giles, London, 1847, 113-4.

16 Asser's description of Athelney: Asser, p.103. Asser's account of the place – where the fortifications were greatly strengthened by Alfred after, as thanksgiving for his victory, he founded the monastery there – are supported by the work of Channel 4's 'Time Team'. The 'Time Team' broadcast, the programme's 100th, was directed and produced by Graham Dixon, and presented by Tony Robinson. (Video Text Communications Ltd, for Channel 4 Television Corporation, 2003.)

17 'submitted to the Vikings ... except Alfred the king'. Asser, p.83. See *Anglo-Saxon Chronicle*, p.75; Asser, p.83. Asser says those who attacked Chippenham came from Exeter – that 'they left Exeter and went to Chippenham.' From the *Anglo-Saxon Chronicle*, however, it seems they came south-east from across the border in Mercia.

18 Egbert's Stone. Possibly at Kingston Deverill, to the south of Warminster in Wiltshire. See ASC, p.76.

19 Bratton Castle. In the late 1600s a white horse was carved on the hillside at Bratton, by way of commemorating the Saxon victory. (It was believed that the Saxons had first brought Christianity to Britain, and that a white horse was a symbol of the triumph over paganism.)

20 'persevered resolutely ... for a long time.' Asser, p.83.

21 'adopted son' : Asser pp.84-85.

2: Aethelflaed and Her Sisters

22 'Often her beauty wanes.' Exeter Book A, 62-64.

23 'a base from which to explore ... 'For a psychotherapist's discussion of a child's need for 'affectionate and responsive' parenting, see J. Bowlby, *A secure base: Parent-child attachment and healthy human development*, New York, 1988: 'Given ... a secure base from which to explore the world and to which to return when in difficulty, it is more than likely that [the child] will grow up to be a cheerful, socially cooperative, and effective citizen, and to be unlikely to break down in adversity.' (p.178.)

24 centrality of women ... education. For the story of Alfred and the reading contest: Asser pp. 90-91.

25 some significant role in the world. Both Alfred and Ealhswith saw to it that their daughters were as well-educated as their sons. Edward and Aelfthryth, Aethelflaed's younger siblings, learned at the royal court, under 'the solicitous care of tutors and nurses', as Bishop Asser explains; and we may assume that Aethelflaed in her time had done the same.

(Only Aethelweard, Edward's younger brother, went to school.) All the children learned to read in English – particularly the Psalms, and 'English poems'. As young adults, they 'very frequently' referred to books,' we are told. Asser, p.90.

26 'a chaste widow'. Asser, p.88. Ealhswith's main claim to fame is her founding of a nunnery, the Nunnaminster at Winchester (later called St Mary's Abbey), with the proceeds from the estates Alfred bequeathed to her in his will.

27 embroider beautifully … the ravages of time. Simeon of Durham gives an eloquent description of the embroidered vestments of St Cuthbert, found when the saint's tomb was opened some years after his death. They were, he says, 'incomparable' in their 'workmanship and worth' (pp.782-3).

28 'dismissed from … sexual service'. The term is Mary Dockray-Miller's, in *Motherhood and Mothering in Anglo-Saxon England*, New York, 2000, p.47.

29 whether … into exile at Athelney … quite likely. For the legend about Alfred and his mother at Athelney, see Chapter 1.

30 'cloaked in silence'. See P. Stafford, 'The King's Wife in Wessex, 800-1066'. In *New Readings on Women in Old English Literature,* ed. H. Damico and A. Hennessy-Olsen, Bloomington, Indiana, 1990, pp. 56-78.

31 Queen Aethelswith's ring is discussed in Dockray-Miller, p.48.

32 For the West Saxon tradition regarding the wife of a king, as deplored by Bishop Asser: pp.71-2.

33 'king's mother': Dockray-Miller points out that the Wessex custom persisted into the reign of Alfred's son Edward, whose wife Aelflaed, when witnessing a charter, is recorded as just that: 'conjunx regis'. (p.48.)

34 For the story of Eadburh: Asser, pp. 71-72

35 'Often her beauty wanes'. See Note 1.

36 monastic lands as their own. For fuller discussion of this point: B.Yorke, '"Sisters Under the Skin"?: Anglo-Saxon nuns and nunneries in southern England', *Reading Medieval Studies* 15, 1989, pp.95-117.

37 The highest ideal for women. Discussed in Aldhelm's 'Treatise on Virginity'. In *Aldhem*, ed. and trans. M. Lapidge and M. Herren, Woodbridge 1999. Cited in Yorke, p.101.

38 For a thoughtful discussion of marriage among the clergy in Anglo-Saxon society, see Catherine Cubitt, 'Images of St Peter: The Clergy and the Religious Life in Anglo-Saxon England.' In P. Cavill, ed., *The Christian Tradition in Anglo-Saxon England: Approaches to Current Scholarship and Teaching*. Cambridge, 2004, pp. 41-54. 'Some of those responsible for the cure of souls may not have lived in religious communities, but rather as a family unit.'

39 Queen Wealtheow. In *Beowulf*, ed. and trans. L. Hall, Chicago, 1892.

40 'She shall be cheerful … to the hand of the lord …' Exeter Book A, 62-64.

41 Asser, p.73.

42 Wellow in Hampshire. Or possibly a different Wellow, in Somerset. See Notes on King Alfred's Will, in Keynes and Lapidge, p.32.

43 Freeing a slave. Quoted in Reynolds, *Later Anglo-Saxon England: Life and Landscape*. Stroud, 1999, p.61.

44 Juliana's martyrdom: The legend of Juliana became the subject of a late tenth-century poem, possibly by Cynewulf.

45 'Judith', transl. Aaron K. Hostetter, https://anglosaxonpoetry.camden. rutgers.edu/ Arman (2017) has suggested that 'Judith' was written in honour of – even commissioned by – Aethelflaed herself in adulthood, as a way of promoting the heroic reputation of the Lady of the Mercians. However, without being too literal-minded about it, it has to be noted that Aethelflaed to our knowledge never personally beheaded anyone; and the date of the poem's composition has been estimated to be as early as the eighth century (and as late as the tenth).

46 Cynewulf, 'Elene', in the Vercelli Book. Transl. Aaron K. Hostetter, https://anglosaxonpoetry.camden.rutgers.edu/

47 Wandering holy men. For the story of one group of these, see ASC p.82; and chapter 5, 'Lady of the Church'.

3: Marriage

48 'as rulers together.' Exeter Book, 22.

49 deputise for the king. For an overview of social ranks in Anglo-Saxon society in the late ninth and tenth centuries, see A. Reynolds, *Later Anglo-Saxon England: Life and Landscape*, Stroud, 1999, pp.58-63.

50 The charter in which Aethelred acknowledges Alfred as his overlord is described in Keynes and Lapidge, Alfred, p.256, note 145. See also Walker, p.69.

51 Vikings in Gloucester. Aethelweard's version of the ASC. (See Walker, p.69.)

52 'praying men ... his ability known'. King Alfred's translation of Boethius's *Consolation of Philosophy*, Section 17. In Keynes and M. Lapidge, pp. 132-3.

53 He sacked ... retraining. Described in Asser, pp. 109-10.

54 lovelorn suitor. See, for example, Annie Whitehead's novel, *To Be a Queen*, FeedARead.com, 2015; and similar examples in my chapter 8.

55 Like the Welsh kings allegedly oppressed by Aethelred, Asser opted to be 'obedient to the royal will'. p.96.

56 considered the material needs ... regularly paid. Reynolds cites an entry from the Domesday Book that seems to relate to the pre-Norman period.

It states that twenty shillings were paid (four shillings from each of five hides), for any man fighting in the service of the king. The money 'was not sent to the king, but was given to the soldiers.' (p.85.)

57 offered his niece valuable moral support. For this insight, I am indebted to Joanna Arman, in *The Warrior Queen*, Stroud, 2017, p.13.

58 disturbing portents. Told in ASC for 896, pp. 76, 89; for 903, p.93; for 904, pp. 92, 94.

59 'Ingimund ... came to Aethelflaed.' *Fragmentary Annals of Ireland*, ed. J. Radner, Dublin, 1978, p.171.

60 A grant to Bishop Waerferth of property in London. For details of the building on the London waterfront, see Stansbury, *The Lady Who Fought the Vikings*, p.117.

61 A charter in Worcester. It is possible, as Jeremy Haslam argues, that the 'new' burh at Worcester was in fact an extension of one built by King Alfred around 880. That would make Worcester one of the first places in England to be fortified; but apparently with a need to increase the burh's extent some fifteen years later, 'for the *protection of all the people*' [Emphasis mine]. See J. Haslam, 'King Alfred, Mercia and London, 874-886: a reassessment', *Anglo-Saxon Studies in Archaeology and History* 17, 2011, pp. 121-46.

62 Another charter in Worcester: http://worcestercathedrallibrary.blogspot.co.uk/2012/03/thelfld-lady-of-mercians-d-918.html   Two manuscript copies of the charter are in the British Library. The version referred to here, from the Worcester Cathedral website, is from Sean Miller, Anglo-Saxons.net

63 To plan the rebuilding of London. See Stansbury, pp. 117, 227; Walker, p.200.

64 In William of Malmesbury, *Chronicle of the Kings of England. From the earliest period to the reign of King Stephen, e*d. J.A. Giles, London: Bohn, 1847.

65 ASC, p.96. Who actually led the Mercian troops at Tettenhall, is an open question. Walker thinks it would have been Aethelred; but if we believe the Fragmentary Annals, with their claim that Aethelred was already ill as early as 902, this seems unlikely.

4: Remaking Mercia

66 For the protection of all the people. See Chapter 3, 'Marriage', for 'a charter in Worcester' for fortifying the town.

67 depriving Mercia. Paul Hill believes that Edward took over the Mercian lands 'for strategic reasons and with the support of his sister.' (*Age of*

Athelstan, p.88.) This makes Edward sound more disinterested, and Aethelflaed happier to cooperate with her brother's plans, than may have been the case.

68 Ingimund enlisted some Danes: *Fragmentary Annals*, p.171.

69 'gave up the city, and left.' FA, p.174.

70 In the rear of the fighting. In S. Pollington, *Tamworth: The Ancient Capital of Mercia,* Tamworth, 2011.

71 'Aethelflaed's fame ... spread.' FA, p.182.

72 A figure of 4,650ft. *The Defence of Wessex: The Burghal Hidage and Anglo-Saxon Fortresses,* ed. D. Hill and A.R. Rumble, Manchester, 1996, pp.226-7.

73 A new garrison would relieve them. Reynolds, p.85.

74 The fortification of Oxford. There are credible grounds 'to support the contention', according to Reynolds (p.90), that Oxford was one of the burhs founded by Aethelflaed and Aethelred.

75 Bremesbyrig, Scergeat, Bridgnorth: ASC pp. 94, 96.

76 Tamworth: ASC for 913, pp. 96, 97.

77 For the industries that developed at Stafford, see M. Carver, in *Stafford Field Reports 1975-1990* (ADS), March 2009.

78 Warwick, 'that summer of 914': ASC, p.98.

79 'meaningless repentance': Asser, p.102. The 'half-made' burh is mentioned in ASC, p.84.

80 'They cornered the Viking force ... leave King Edward's domain.' ASC for 914, p.98. (Mercia was, of course, a sub-kingdom of Edward's Wessex.)

81 over the Mersey narrows. ASC, p.99.

82 the burh at Wednesbury. For a description of Steve Field's commemorative sculpture of Aethelflaed in Wednesbury, see chapter 8.

83 The queen of Brecon Mere. ASC, p.100.

84 The clue ... lies with the queen's husband at Brecon Mere. See *Caradoc of Llancarvan: The History of Wales,* trans. D. Powell and W. Wynne, London, 1774; reprinted,Shrewsbury, 1832, p.46.

85 Huganus. Caradoc, pp. 46-77.

86 A well-guarded burh. ASC, p.101.

87 'chose Edward as their lord ...'. ASC, pp. 102-3.

88 'took possession of the stronghold.' ASC, p.101.

89 'the raiding-armies ... subjected.' ASC, p.105.

90 The term *thegn* covered a range of ranks and occupations. Originally, it had denoted a high-ranking servant of the king – 'normally the household officer of a great man'. While this role persisted, by the tenth century a thegn might also be a fighting man in the king's service; or either a small

or a hugely wealthy landowner. One of these, a man named Wulfric Spott, by AD1004 owned seventy-two estates across Mercia and even in parts of the Danelaw. See Reynolds, p.59.

91 Kingsholm palace: Hurst, H. et al. 'Excavations at Gloucester: Third Interim Report, Kingsholm 1966-75', *Antiquaries Journal* 55.2 (September 1975), pp. 274, 284.

92 business with the Continent. See Walker, p.200.

93 upkeep of the royal horses. Described in Walker, p.201.

94 'Aethelflaed ... cleverness'. FA, pp. 181-82.

95 The Hundreds, which by law required the attendance of a representative of each of a hundred hides of land – one man from each of a hundred families – met monthly. Presided over by a local official known as a reeve, it functioned as a combination of magistrates' court, ad hoc police force for pursuing cattle raiders, and parish council. The shire courts heard appeals from judgments handed down at the Hundred. For more information on the tenth-century Anglo-Saxon court system, from the local Hundred courts, through the shire courts to the system of appeal to the ruler, see Reynolds, p.99.

96 Coins ... ceased to be produced. Karkov offers a thought-provoking discussion of these coins in 'Aethelflaed's Exceptional Coinage?' *Old English Newsletter* 29.1, 1995, p.41.

97 A ruling that may have extended to Mercia. See Reynolds, p.174.

98 Ten per cent ... town dwellers. Reynolds, p.57. According to Reynolds, 'In the West and South Midlands, shires were organised around newly built fortified towns or re-fortified centres, with the shires taking the names of the settlements... their dependent towns nearly always centrally placed'. (p.75.) The shire may originally have had a military function, supplying troops and provisions to its central burh town.

99 Celebrations in her memory. For an account of commemorations in Tamworth and other Mercian 'burh' towns, see chapter 8.

5: Lady of the Church

100 'the reward of eternal bliss'. The contract in Worcester leasing land to Aethelred and Aethelflaed. Robertson, *Charters*, 19, pp. 34-39.

101 disobey God's commands. See, for example the Blickling Homilies, written in the late ninth century. The quotations are from the homily for the First and Fifth Sundays in Lent. In *Blickling Homilies*, trans. R. Morris. Cambridge, Ontario, 2000, pp. 18, 29.

102 daughters ... literate in religious matters. Asser, pp. 65-110. Asser tells us that Alfred's younger children, Edward and Aelfthryth, who presumably were still at an age for schooling when he first met them in

about 885, had 'attentively learned the Psalms, and books in English.' (p.91.) Aethelflaed, by then an adolescent on the threshold of marriage, or possibly already married, would have received a similar education.

103 distant relatives ... marry ... Issues discussed in G. R. Owen, *Rites and Religions of the Anglo-Saxons*, Totowa, New Jersey, 1981. Thompson, in her *Dying and Death in Later Anglo-Saxon England*, (Woodbridge, 2003, p.63), highlights the diversity apparent in the instructions of local religious authorities – for example, regarding rites of preparation for the sick and dying.

104 The pope sent Alfred a fragment ... crucified. Asser, p.93.

105 corresponds with Fulco: 'The Letter of Fulco, archbishop of Rheims, to King Alfred', in Keynes and Lapidge, pp. 182-86.

106 'pilgrims ... pro amore dei'. The three holy men, and their visit to King Alfred, are described in the ASC for 891, p.82, and in Asser, pp. 113-4.

107 psychosomatic ... anxious prayer. Asser, pp.89-90.

108 Lands to be saved ... Vikings. Walker, *Mercia and the Making of England*, Stroud, 2000, p.200.

109 'He would not forsake divine service.' Asser, p.79. See also chapter 6, 'Alfred's Daughter'.

110 a kingdom ... devout men and women. See the Preface to Alfred's translation of Gregory's *Pastoral Care*, in Keynes and Lapidge, p.125. As the editors observe: 'In common with many Christian authors before and after him, Alfred regarded the invasion of hostile peoples as a form of divine punishment for decadence and decay.' (Note 6, p.295.)

111 writing as a woman. So, for instance, the scribe writes 'inconcusam' [sic] (= unshaken), where the masculine form, 'inconcussum' might be expected. The original prayer book is in the keeping of the British Library (Harley MS 2965). Reproduced as a facsimile in W. De Gray Birch, *An Ancient Manuscript of the Eighth or Ninth Century Formerly Belonging to St Mary's Abbey, or Nunnaminster,* London, 1889.

112 unworthiness before God...'everlasting rejoicing'. Quoted in De Gray Birch, *Ancient Manuscript*, pp.88, 77.

113 The 'Royal Manuscript'. De Gray Birch, citing Harley MS 7653, in *Ancient Manuscript,* p.117.

114 Magical charms or spells. For a detailed exploration of this topic: Jolly, K. L. *Popular Religion In `Late Saxon England: Elf Charms In Context*, Chapel Hill and London, 1996.

115 'The Lord is our protection...' Psalm 9. 2-3, p.155; Psalm 45.1, in Alfred's version. Keynes and Lapidge, p.159.

116 Saint Andrew. In Blickling Homily 19, Andrew, persecuted and ill-treated for his faith, is represented as standing firm: 'Though you kill me, yet will I not do your will, but I will do that of my Lord Jesus Christ.' (p.120.)

117 Christ as a young warrior. 'The Dream of the Rood,' Exeter Book.
Transl. Mark Leech, http://www.stephen-spender.org/2004_prize/ssmt_
evPrizeOver18_01.htm

118 'To us God is everlasting ...' Exeter Book A, 8-12.

119 'manifold ... customs.' Exeter A, 12-18.

120 'they that preach peace ... ' Exeter A, 20-21.

121 not Christians. In the ASC Vikings are regularly alluded to as 'the heathen',
and the Anglo-Saxons as 'the Christians' – pp. 67, 87, for example.

122 'with the symbol of the cross'. Robertson, *Charters*, 19, pp. 34-39.

123 land boundary disputes: In 899, a priest named Waerferth (a different
man from the bishop of that name), got into a dispute with a fellow priest,
Aethelwold, over the ownership of land at Woodchester. Lord Aethelred
of the Mercians was called upon to sort the matter out. The story is told in
Walker, p.184.

124 'Loathed is he who lays claim ... donates more.' Exeter A, 58.

125 'give gold away.' 'Gold mon sceal gifan ... ' : Exeter C, 18-19.

126 'God loveth a cheerful giver', Asser's *Life,* p.106. Asser refers to
Corinthians II. 9.7: Let each one give just as he has decided in his heart,
not grudgingly or under compulsion, for God loves a cheerful giver.'

127 The New Minster ... St Peter. Confusingly, there was already a church
nearby named St Peter's, that later was rebuilt on a grander scale as
Gloucester Cathedral. For 'secular canons', see D. Dunford, 'Canon'.
in *The Catholic Encyclopedia.* New York, 1908, http://www.newadvent.
org/cathen/03252a.htm

128 the family mausoleum. Thompson, in her *Dying and Death in Later
Anglo-Saxon England*, Woodbridge, 2002, believes that Aethelred and
Aethelflaed made 'a conscious decision' not to 'fall in with West Saxon
plans for the new royal mausoleum at Winchester.' (p.14.) If, on the
other hand, building a church and a mausoleum at Tamworth might have
looked to the royal house of Wessex like a renewed claim to Mercian
sovereignty, then possibly the choice of Gloucester offered 'a middle
way'.

129 a blessing to 'flow' there. Bintley, 'The translation of St Oswald's relics to
New Minster, Gloucester: royal and imperial resonances', *Anglo-Saxon
Studies in Archaeology and History* 19, 2014, pp. 171-81.

130 Oswald's body ... uncorrupted. 'Is it cynical to suppose that the bodies of
potential saints were embalmed in some way? 'asks Owen, in *Rites and
religions of the Anglo-Saxons.*

131 her father's maternal ancestors. See Thompson, p.14.

132 'an incredible step forward in the ... city.' Talk given by Chris Chatterton
at Gloucester Museum, for the Gloucester History Festival in

August 2014. An enthusiastic member of Chatterton's audience added, only half-jokingly, 'She actually founded the tourist trade in Gloucester, if you think about it.'

133 For an evocative description of Aethelflaed's Gloucester, including St Oswald's and the Kingsholm Palace, see Heighway, *Gloucester: A History and Guide,* Gloucester 1985, pp. 29-38.

134 founded a church ... Churchdown. A tradition recorded by Gwen Waters, in *The Story of Churchdown, Gloucestershire: A Village History.* London,1999, p.26. For a description of the stained glass window in Churchdown that commemorates this event, see chapter 8.

135 She had the churches there rebuilt. For a summary of these restorations: Walker, p.196.Also P. Courtney, *Saxon and Medieval Leicester: The Making of an Urban Landscape*, Leicester, 1998, p.132. First published as an article in *Transactions of the Leicestershire Archaeological and Historical Society*, 73, 1998, pp. 110-45.

136 the nunnery ... Wenlock. For an account of the land grant, and the charter authorising it: M. Gelling, *The West Midlands in the Middle Ages*, Leicester, 1992, p.164.

137 St Bertelin's. See H.F. Starkey (1990), *Old Runcorn*, Halton, 1990. See also N. J. Higham, *The Origins of Cheshire*, Manchester, 1993, p.111; and Edward Watson, http://clasmerdin.blogspot.co.uk/ 2013. Accessed November 2016. Watson observes that 'the dedication of what was almost certainly a new church there to St Bertelin [Beorhthelm] at Runcorn suggests Æthelflæd's responsibility.' Watson believes she would have recently been in contact with what he calls 'this obscure Mercian cult', when building the new burh at Stafford just two years earlier.

6: Alfred's Daughter

138 'Daughters whose fathers ... males': Nielsen, http//:family-studies.org/ how-dads-affect-their-`daughters-into-adulthood/ A father's influence will 'serve as an examplefor his daughter ... in her `own life, even if she chooses a different view of the world'. Austin. M, quoted in E. Weiss-`McGolerick, 'The importance of the father-daughter relationship', *Parenting*, 11 October 2012.

139 'I could not as my father's daughter remain indifferent ...' Aung San Suu Kyi, Burmese democracy activist and national political leader, daughter of assassinated president Bogyoke Aung San. In her first public speech, 26 August 1988.

140 encouragement from her father. See Nielsen, *Father-Daughter Relationships: Contemporary Research and Issues*, New York, 2012, pp.74-83.

Alfred's Preface to Bishop Waerferth's translation of Gregory's *Dialogues*. Keynes and Lapidge, pp.125-6.

141 'fought against seven ship-loads ... 'ASC, 867-874, pp. 69-74.

142 '... he did not think that he alone ... ferocity... 'Asser, p.81.

143 'like a wild boar'. Asser, p.79.

144 'to reflect on heavenly things ... earthly tribulations'. Alfred's Preface to Bishop Waerferth's translation of Gregory's *Dialogues*. Keynes and Lapidge, p.123.

145 'to arrive ... whence you formerly came'. Alfred's additional comments, in his translation of Boethius, *Consolation of Philosophy*, 27.2. In Keynes and Lapidge, pp.133, 135.

146 Prayers for their souls. For instance, as described in my chapter 5, 'Lady of the Church', Aethelflaed and Aethelred's grant of land to the nunnery of St Mildburh, in return for the prayers of the community there.

147 Women who have grown up without a brother 'are overly represented among the world's political leaders: they tend to receive more encouragement from their fathers to be high achievers'. 'He hopes others will do better ... 'Asser, p.92. Alfred asks readers 'not to blame' him, in his preface to Boethius' *Consolation of Philosophy,* p.132.

148 'before everything was ransacked and burned'. Alfred's Preface to Bishop Waerferth's translation of Gregory's *Dialogues*. Keynes and Lapidge, pp.125-6.

149 Aethelweard: Asser, p.91.

150 'for fear of being turned out of office'. Asser, p.110.

151 Each of the tools ... wishes to use. Preface to Alfred's translation of Augustine's *Soliloquies*. In Keynes and Lapidge, p.138.

152 Candles burning ... prayer: Asser, pp. 101, 108.

153 captured Viking ships. ASC, p.90.

154 Aelfwynn: witnessing of legal documents. For the document-witnessing episode, see Dockray-Miller, p.71. The signature of a teenage Aelfwynn appears witnessing a charter in which her uncle King Edward records a land grant, 'from Aethulf to his daughter Aethelgyth'.

155 Appointing an abbot ... Athelney: Asser, p.105.

156 'challenging him gently': Asser, pp.101-2, 109.

157 a royal command: Preface to Alfred's translation of *Gregory's Pastoral Care*. In Keynes and Lapidge, p.126.

158 'enriched ... with honour and authority'. Asser, pp. 91, 103.

159 Women who have grown up without a brother 'are overly represented among the world's political leaders: they tend to receive more encouragement from their fathers to be high achievers'.

160 a certain amount of tension … Edward. See Paul Hill, *The Age of Athelstan: Britain's Forgotten History*, Stroud, 2004, p.88. A point discussed in detail in chapter 7.

161 'to live worthily'.In Alfred's translation of Boethius, Keynes and Lapidge, p.133.

7: Aethelflaed's (Missing) Daughter

162 'her brother … nervous': Dockray-Miller, *Motherhood and Mothering in Anglo-Saxon England*, p.59.

163 Leicester … surrendered. ASC, p.105.

164 The tensions … rising to the surface. See Paul Hill, *The Age of Athelstan: Britain's Forgotten History*, Stroud, 2004, p.88: 'We need not necessarily assume that the two allied commanders, Edward and Aethelflaed, saw eye-to-eye on military and political issues, as anyone who has read about the struggles between Dwight D. Eisenhower and Field Marshal Montgomery will be aware.'

165 She 'departed … midsummer'. ASC, p.103.

166 recite the Laudate Dominum daily. Walker, p.112. (See also chapter 5.)

167 … bears Aelfwynn's signature. See note to p.100. 'if Aelfwynn survives them …' For this Worcester charter: Robertson, *Charters*, no. 19, pp. 34-9.

168 '… and turned to him'. ASC, p.103.

169 'deprived … carried into Wessex'. ASC, p.105.

170 'most ungratefully disinherited …' *Caradoc of Llancarvan: The History of Wales*, Transl. Dr Powell and W. Wynne. London, 1774; Shrewsbury, 1832, pp. 39-40. See also my chapter 4, 'Lady of the Mercians'.

171 Suggested that Edward met … witan. By Walker, for instance, p.113.

172 Women were subject to these patriarchal norms. Yorke comments (p.105) that, given the limitations on women's rights to permanently own or bequeath land, 'Family rights over land were a problem for the church throughout the Anglo-Saxon period. 'The problem affected male religious houses too, but in Yorke's view was 'particularly acute with nunneries'.

173 'contracted marriage … Danes'. Caradoc, pp. 39-40.

174 finally provoked him to to depose her. Hill expresses puzzlement over Edward's seeming delay in deposing Aelfwynn: 'What is extraordinary about the Aelfwynn affair is not that Edward ordered an abduction of his niece, but the time it appears to have taken him.' (p.97.)

175 Athelstan … singled out for favour. William of Malmesbury tells this story, while recounting Athelstan's accession to the throne in 924. *Chronicle of the Kings of England,* 131.

176 little better than a foreign invader. 'For many of the inhabitants [of Chester] Edward was as "foreign" a ruler as any Welsh or Scandinavian petty king or

warlord. The received impression is one of an assimilated local population uniting against a distant and repressive royal authority ...' D. Griffith, 'The North-West Frontier', in *Edward the Elder: 899-824,* ed. N.J. Higham and D. H. Hill, London, 2013, pp. 182-3.

177 the well-known statue. By Edward George Bramwell – unveiled in 1913 to commemorate Aethelflaed's building of the burh at Tamworth. See chapter 8.

178 list ... Nunnaminster. The list of 'Nomina Feminarum Illustrium' compiled by the abbot of the Nunnaminster at Winchester in his *Liber Vitae* of 1031, which 'includes the name Aelfwynn, with no epithet to describe her'. Dockray-Miller, p.75.

179 'a different sort of success'. Dockray-Miller, pp. 74-76.

8: Legend and Legacy

180 'of equal service in building cities ... able to protect men at home, and to intimidate them abroad': 'William of Malmesbury's *Chronicle of the Kings of England: from the earliest period to the reign of `King Stephen,* ed. J.A. Giles, Bohn, 1847. 'kicked Viking butt': Sacre Brew advertisement for Aethelflaed ale. (See note to p.132, below.) 'Unconquerable queen'. Henry of Huntingdon's phrase, in a poem translated from the Latin by Francis Peck, in his *History of Stafford. (Academia Tertia Anglicana, or The Antiquities of Stafford,* London, 1727.)

181 'of singular virtues': *Caradoc of Llancarvan: The History of Wales,* trans. D. Powell and W. Wynne. London, 1774; reprinted Shrewsbury, 1832, pp. 38-40.

182 'Famosissima regina': *The Annals of Ulster,* eds. D. O Corrain, M. Cournane, Cork, 2005 / 2008 https://www.ucc.ie/celt/online/G100001A. html U918.5, p.366.

183 Known Aethelflaeds after 918. Listed in E.Van Houts, *Memory and Gender in Medieval Europe, 900-1200,* London, 1999, p.104. (See also Walker, pp.119-20.)

184 'O potent Elfleda!' Henry of Huntingdon's phrase, in his poem translated from the Latin by Francis Peck, in his *History of Stafford. (Academia Tertia Anglicana, or The Antiquities of Stafford,* London, 1727.)

185 William of Malmesbury's *Chronicle of the Kings of England: from the earliest period to the reign of King Stephen,* ed. J.A. Giles, Bohn, 1847.

186 Matilda ... Stephen. For this insight, I am indebted to Wolfe, who draws on Weir, *Britain's Royal Families* (London, 1989), for her account of Matilda's war with Stephen. See J.Wolfe, *Royal Lady, War Lady,* Chester, 2001, p.19.

187 administrator of a kingdom. Aethelflaed, in the Cartulary and Customs of Abingdon Abbey, c.1220.

188 confused with … Aethelgifu: Æthelflæd, from a thirteenth-century genealogical chronicle (London, British Library, MS Royal 14 B V). For digitalised reproductions of this image, and that in Note 10: http://blogs. bl.uk/digitisedmanuscripts/2013/08/the-lady-of-the-mercians.html

189 'La Sage'. Æthelflæd, from a fourteenth-century genealogical chronicle. (London, British Library, MS Royal 14B VI.)

190 idealised Alfred's reign. See John Spelman: *The Life of Alfred the Great from the Manuscripts in the Bodleian Library: With considerable additions and several historical remarks by the Publisher, Thomas Hearne,* Oxford, 1707. Spelman, a moderate Royalist with Protestant sympathies, completed the first (unpublished) version of his biography in 1642, on the eve of the English Civil War. Parker, in her *England's Darling: The Victorian Cult of Alfred the Great* (Manchester, 2007), offers a comprehensive study of the meaning of Spelman's work for Victorian ideas about the King: pp. 57-61, and *passim*.

191 an anonymous play … eighteenth century. *Alfred the Great; deliverer of his country. A tragedy,* London, 1753; reprinted in Ecco edition, 2017.

192 Paul de Rapin (Rapin de Thoyras), *The History of England*, ed. and trans. N. Tindall, 2nd edn, vol. 1, London, 1732, p.98.

193 The Alfred millenary tableaux. Described in D. Horspool, *Why Alfred Burned the Cakes: A King and His Eleven-Hundred-Year Afterlife,* London, 2007, pp. 32, 159.

194 Ethelfleda Mound. In 'Compendium of County History: Staffordshire', *Gentleman's Magazine* 93. ii, July 1823, pp. 23- 27.

195 the company refused. Told in D. Thompson, *Bridging the Mersey: A Pictorial History*, Zaltbommel, 2000.

196 The pioneer … Warwick. Parker produced a souvenir brochure with a slightly misleading title: L. Parker, *The Warwick Pageant, July 2-7, 1906. In Celebration of the Thousandth Anniversary of the Conquest of Mercia by Queen Ethelfleda,* Warwick, 1906.

197 Stafford pageant. A. Bartie et al, 'Stafford Millenary Pageant: The Redress of the Past.http://www.historicalpageants.ac.uk/pageants/1203/

198 'Have we forgotten a big anniversary?' In *Tamworth Herald,* 18 January 2013. http://www.tamworthherald.co.uk/forgotten-big-anniversary/story-17892962-detail/story.html ; 'Millenary of Tamworth Castle: The Celebration. Wonderful Success', *The Herald,* 12 July 1913, pp. 5,8.

199 Woodville's scenes of Aetheflaed's attack on Llangorse (Brecon Mere) In *Hutchinson's Story of the `British Nation : a connected, pictorial & authoritative history of the British peoples from the earliest `times to the present day,* ed. W. Hutchinson, London, 1922.

200 dance production. 'Tigress; Warrior Queen returns to Tamworth Castle', 16 April 2015. http://www.bbc.co.uk/programmes/articles/1QgD6KT7lCJT7K2vWW7jBn9/tigress-warrior-queen-returns-to-tamworth-castle April 16, 2015. Accessed on 20 November, 2016.

201 a grey-eyed, serious Aethelflaed: http://historysheroes.e2bn.org/

202 mounted astride: https://weaponsandwarfare.com/2016/02/24/aethelflaed/

203 A Quick Concept Drawing: 'Aethelflaed of Mercia, 917 AD' httpgambargin.deviantart.comartAethelflaed-of-Mercia-917-AD-Women-War-Queens-462760526

204 'as if for a pleasant day's riding ...' In S. Pollington, *Tamworth: The Ancient Capital of Mercia*, Tamworth, 2011.

205 'Cool Chicks from History': https://chibisketches.wordpress.com/2014/06/20/cool-chicks-from-history-2/

206 Aethelflaed as dreamy-looking female. 'Aethelflaed' by 'Edriss': https://uk.pinterest.com/explore/edriss-deviantart/This, and most of the other Internet images described in *Founder, Fighter, Saxon Queen*, can still be found online.

207 a gnome-like figure – Aethelflaed as 'Hobbit': Lupi McGinty: http: //www.lupiloops.combooks-and-prints

208 Disney-style princess: http: //tigertwins.deviantart.com/art/Aethelflaed-3954899781

209 'Marasop': http://marasop.deviantart.com/http://marasop.deviantart.com/

210 tattooed arms... breast: http://alchetron.com/AEthelflaed-736698-W (No longer online.)

211 Ignis Antiquita. Aromaleigh: https://aromaleighv2.files.wordpress.com/2013/12/aethelflaed-grid.jpg Posted 24 December 2013.

212 Medieval war games. Bad Squiddo Games: https://thedicebaglady.net/bad-squiddo-games-aethelflaed-lady-of-mercia-pack-of-2/

213 José Carmona's design for Sacre Brew: http://www.sacrebrew.com/2014/04/?thelfl?d

214 A number of novelists: Haley Garwood, *Swords Across the Thames*, Bruceton Mills, 1999; Marjory Grieser, *King Alfred's Daughter*, Indianapolis, 2009; Penny Ingham, *The King's Daughter*, Farnham, 2010; Rebecca Tingle, *The Edge on the Sword*, New York, 2001; Annie Whitehead, *To Be a Queen*, FeedARead.com, 2015.

215 Cornwell's 'Anglo-Saxon Stories'. All published in London by Harper Collins.

216 'mightily unfair' to Aethelred. Cornwell's note on his characters, at the end of *The Burning Land*. `p.382.

217 She hears the people praising her courage: pp.272-3

218 'he had fallen in love with her.' *The King's Daughter*, p.222.

219 'a creature of gold'. *The Burning Land*, p.266.

220 A Viking ambush. *To Be a Queen*, p.101. Thanks to the Internet, this fictional episode in Whitehead's novel, is on its way to becoming, if not historical fact, at least part of the Aethelflaed legend. See Arman's *The Warrior Queen,* p.188.

221 'eating Viking herring'. *To Be a Queen*, p.397.

222 Disinherits Aelfwynn: 'Take my name out of history.' In *Swords Across the Thames*, p.404.

223 'mischief and life and laughter'. *The Burning Land*, p.258.

224 'None of you have the courage …' In *Sword Song*, p.119.

225 'curdled': p.258

226 'reading your thoughts and despising them.' *The Empty Throne*, p.19.

227 check the … stores … buckets of mud. See, for example, *To Be a Queen*, pp. 230, 353.

228 *The Last Kingdom,* TV dramatisation. The series first aired in the UK on BBC Two in October 2015.

229 his ground-breaking essay: F. T. Wainwright, 'Aethelflaed Lady of the Mercians' in *The Anglo-Saxons: Studies in Some Aspects of their History and Culture, presented to Bruce Dickins*. Clemoes, P., (ed.), London, 1959. Reprinted in *New Readings on Women in Old English Literature,* eds Damico and Hennessy-Olsen, Bloomington, 1990.

230 S. Hollis, *Anglo-Saxon Women and the Church*, Woodbridge, 1992, p.236.

231 'a leader … from the saddle.' Hill, *Age of Athelstan*, p.87.

232 'capable of … feats of heroism'. J. Arman, *The Warrior Queen,* Stroud, 2017, p.227.
    Aethelflaed's other skills: Arman, pp. 154-71, p.231.

233 'founding mother'. Holland, *Athelstan*, London 2016.

234 'her goals were … protection'; 'a perceptive and dedicated manager'. Dockray-Miller, pp. 74, 66.

235 'The woman's way': D. Stansbury, *The Lady Who Fought the Vikings*, South Brent, 1993, p.218.
    'the influence of a woman': *The Lady Who Fought the Vikings*, Plymouth, 1993, pp. 178. 198.

236 Fighting 'not a sport': Stansbury, p.210.

237 typical of high-status Anglo-Saxons. Thompson, *Dying and Death in Later Anglo-Saxon England*, Woodbridge, 2002, p.8.

NOTES

Where to Find Her

238 St Leonard's, Bridgnorth. Fragments of Saxon stone incorporated in its walls: S. Marchant, *St Leonard's Church, Bridgnorth*, London, 2001.

239 The palace at Kingsholm: 'H. Hurst, et al., 'Excavations at Gloucester: Third Interim Report, Kingsholm 1966-75', *Antiquaries Journal* 55.2 (September 1975), p.274. (Published online, 29 November 2011.)

240 Saxon defences at Hereford. See R. Shoesmith, 'Hereford Saxon defences', *Current Archaeology* 3, 1971, pp 256-8. See also http://www.buildingstones.org.uk/about/

241 Founded or rebuilt by Aethelflaed. P. Courtney, *Saxon and Medieval Leicester: The Making of an Urban Landscape,* Leicester, 1998, p.132. First published as an article in Transactions of the Leicestershire Archaeological and Historical Society, 73, 1998, pp. 110-45.

242 said to have been one of the earliest Mercian burhs. On the basis of a charter signed by Aethelred and Aethelflaed at Shrewsbury in 901, after a meeting there of the Mercian witan. Stansbury, p.152-3.

243 Saxon 'market cross' of main streets in Stafford: M. Carver, *The Birth of a Borough: An Archaeological Study of Anglo-Saxon Stafford*, Woodbridge 2010, pp. 74, 99-100.

Bibliography

Primary Sources

Abbo of Fleury's 'Life of St. Edmund, King of East Anglia', ed. H. Sweet, *Anglo-Saxon Primer*, 9th edn, trans. K. Cutler, Oxford, 1961.

Academia Tertia Anglicana, or The Antiquities of Stafford, ed. F. Peck, London, 1727.

Aldhelm: The Prose Works, ed. M. Lapidge and M. Herren, Cambridge, 1979.

An Ancient Manuscript of the Eighth or Ninth Century Formerly Belonging to St Mary's Abbey, or Nunnaminster, Winchester, ed. W. de Gray Birch, London, 1889.

The Anglo-Saxon Chronicles, (ASC), ed. and trans. M. Swanton, 2nd edn, London, 2001.

Anglo-Saxon Charters, ed. and trans. A.J. Robertson, Cambridge, 1939.

The Annals of Ulster, eds. D.O. Corrain, M. Cournane, Cork, 2005/2008. https://www.ucc.ie/celt/online/G100001A.html

Asser, Life of King Alfred, in *Alfred the Great, Asser's Life of King Alfred and other contemporary sources*, ed. and trans. S. Keynes and M. Lapidge, London, 1983.

Beowulf, ed. and trans. L. Hall, Chicago, 1892.

The Blickling Homilies, trans. R. Morris, Cambridge, Ontario, 2000.

Caradoc of Llancarvan: The History of Wales, trans. D. Powell and W. Wynne, London, 1774; reprinted, Shrewsbury, 1832.

The Chronicle of Aethelweard, ed. A. Campbell, Edinburgh, 1962.

Cynewulf, 'Elene', trans. A. Hostetter, https://anglosaxonpoetry.camden.rutgers.edu/

Cynewulf, 'Juliana', trans. A. Hostetter, https://anglosaxonpoetry.camden.rutgers.edu/

'The Dream of the Rood,' trans. M. Leech, http://www.stephen-spender.org/2004_prize/ssmtevPrizeOver18_01.htm

Fragmentary Annals of Ireland, (FA), ed. J. Radner, Dublin, 1978.

'Judith', transl. Aaron K. Hostetter, https://anglosaxonpoetry.camden.rutgers.edu/

BIBLIOGRAPHY

Cynewulf, 'Elene', in the Vercelli Book. Transl. Aaron K. Hostetter, https://anglosaxonpoetry.camden.rutgers.edu/

Liber Vitae: Register of Martyrology of New Minster and Hyde Abbey, Winchester, ed. W. de Gray and W. Birch, London, 1892.

Simeon of Durham: A History of the Kings of England, ed. and trans. J. Stephenson; reprinted, Lampeter, 1987.

William of Malmesbury, Chronicle of the Kings of England: From the earliest period to the reign of King Stephen, ed. J.A. Giles, London, 1847.

Secondary Sources Books

Alfred the Great; deliverer of his country. A tragedy. Anon, London, 1753, reprinted in Ecco edition, 2017.

Arman, J. *The Warrior Queen: The Life and Legend of Aethelflaed, Daughter of Alfred the Great,* Stroud, 1917.

Bowlby, J. *A secure base: Parent-child attachment and healthy human development*, New York, 1988.

Carver, M. *The Birth of a Borough: An Archaeological Study of Anglo-Saxon Stafford*, Woodbridge, 2010.

Cornwell, B. *The Burning Land,* London, 2009

The Empty Throne, London, 2014

Sword Song, London, 2007

Courtney, P. *Saxon and Medieval Leicester: The Making of an Urban Landscape*, 1998. First published in *Transactions of the Leicestershire Archaeological and Historical Society*, 73, 1998, pp. 110-45.

De Rapin, P. *The History of England*, ed. and trans. N. Tindall, 2nd edn, vol. 1, London, 1732.

Dockray-Miller, M. *Motherhood and Mothering in Anglo-Saxon England*, New York, 2000.

Fell, C. *Women In Anglo-Saxon England*, London, 1984.

Foot, S. *Aethelstan: The First King of England,* New Haven, CT, 2011.

Garwood, H.E. *Swords Across the Thames,* Bruceton Mills, 1999.

Gelling, M. *The West Midlands in the Early Middle Ages*, Leicester, 1992.

Grieser, M.A. *King Alfred's Daughter*, Indianapolis, 2009.

Harris, B.E., and Thacker, A.T. (eds.) *The Victoria History of the County of Cheshire,* vol 1, Oxford, 1987.

Heighway, C., Bryant, R., et al. *The Golden Minster: The Anglo-Saxon Minster and Later Medieval Priory of St Oswald at Gloucester,* York, 1999.

Heighway, C. *Gloucester: A History and Guide,* Gloucester 1985.

Higham, N.J. *The Origins of Cheshire*, Manchester, 1993.

Hill, D., and Rumble, A.R. (eds.) *The Defence of Wessex: The Burghal Hidage and Anglo-Saxon Fortresses*, Manchester, 1996.

Hill, P. *The Age of Athelstan: Britain's Forgotten History*, Stroud, 2004.

Hill, P. *The Viking Wars of Alfred the Great,* Barnsley, 2008.

Holland, T. *Athelstan,* London, 2016.

Hollis, S. *Anglo-Saxon Women and the Church*, Woodbridge, 1992.

Holman, K. *The A to Z of the Vikings*, Lanham, MD, 2009.

Hooke, D. *The Anglo-Saxon Landscape: The Kingdom of the Hwicce*, Manchester, 1985.

Horspool, D. *Why Alfred Burned the Cakes: A King and His Eleven-Hundred-Year Afterlife*, London, 2007.

Hutchinson, W. (ed.) *Hutchinson's Story of the British Nation: a connected, pictorial & authoritative history of the British peoples from the earliest times to the present day,* London, 1922.

Ingham, P. *The King's Daughter,* Farnham, 2010.

Jolly, K.L. *Popular Religion In Late Saxon England: Elf Charms In Context*, Chapel Hill and London, 1996.

Jones, G. *A History of the Vikings,* 2nd edn, Oxford, 1984.

Kirby, D. *The Story of Gloucester,* Stroud, 2007.

Magnusson, M. *Vikings!* New York, 1980.

Marchant, S. *St Leonard's Church, Bridgnorth,* London, 2001.

Nielsen, *Father-Daughter Relationships: Contemporary Research and Issues*, New York, 2012, pp.74-83.

Owen, G. *Rites and Religions of the Anglo-Saxons*, Totowa, New Jersey, 1981.

Parker, J. *'England's Darling': The Victorian Cult of Alfred the Great*, Manchester, 2007.

Parker, L. *The Warwick Pageant, July 2-7, 1906. In Celebration of the Thousandth Anniversary of the Conquest of Mercia by Queen Ethelfleda,* Warwick, 1906.

Pollington, S. *Tamworth: The Ancient Capital of Mercia*, Tamworth, 2011.

Reynolds, A. *Later Anglo-Saxon England: Life and Landscape*, Stroud, 1999.

Spelman, J. *The Life of Alfred the Great from the Manuscripts in the Bodleian Library: With considerable additions and several historical remarks by the Publisher, Thomas Hearne*, Oxford, 1707.

Stansbury, D. *The Lady Who Fought the Vikings*, Plymouth, 1993.

Starkey, H.F. *Old Runcorn*, Halton, 1990.

Stenton. F. *Anglo-Saxon England*, 3rd edn, Oxford, 1971.

Thompson, D. *Bridging the Mersey: A Pictorial History*, Zaltbommel, 2000.

Thompson, V. *Dying and Death in Later Anglo-Saxon England*, Woodbridge, 2002.

Tingle, R. *The Edge on the Sword*, New York, 2001.

Van Houts, E. *Memory and Gender in Medieval Europe, 900-1200*, London, 1999.

BIBLIOGRAPHY

Wainwright, F.T. (ed.) *Scandinavian England*, Chichester, 1975.
Walker, I.W. *Mercia and the Making of England*, Stroud, 2000.
Waters, G. *The Story of Churchdown: A Village History*, London, 1999.
Weir, A. *Britain's Royal Families*, London, 1989.
Whitehead, A. *To Be a Queen*, FeedARead.com, 2015.
Wolfe, J. *Royal Lady, War Lady*, Chester, 2001.

Articles

Bartie, A., et al. 'Stafford Millenary Pageant: The Redress of the Past' http://www.historicalpageants.ac.uk/pageants/1203/

Bintley, M. 'The Translation of St Oswald's Relics to New Minster, Gloucester: royal and imperial resonances' in *Anglo-Saxon Studies in Archaeology and History*, 19, 2014, pp. 171-81.

Carver M. *Stafford Field Reports 1975–1990* (ADS), 2009 http://archaeologydataservice.ac.uk/archives.xhtml

'Compendium of County History – Staffordshire' in *Gentleman's Magazine*, 93 pt 2, July 1823, p.24.

Cubitt, C. 'Images of St Peter: The Clergy and the Religious Life in Anglo-Saxon England' in Cavill (ed.) *The Christian Tradition in Anglo-Saxon England: Approaches to Current Scholarship and Teaching*, Cambridge, 2004, pp.56-78.

Davidson, M. 'The (Non) Submission of the Northern Kings in 920' in Higham and Hill (eds.), *Edward the Elder 899-924*, London, 2001, pp. 200-201.

Dunford, D. 'Canon' in *The Catholic Encyclopedia*, New York, 1908 (Accessed on 10 December 2016, from New Advent: http://www.newadvent.org/cathen/03252a.htm)

Griffith, D. 'The North-West Frontier' in Higham and Hill (eds.), *Edward the Elder 899-924*, London, 2001, pp. 167-87

Haslam, J. 'King Alfred, Mercia and London, 874-886: a reassessment' in *Anglo-Saxon Studies in Archaeology and History*, 17, 2011, pp.121-46.

'Have we forgotten a big anniversary?' *Tamworth Herald*, 18 January 2013. http://www.tamworthherald.co.uk/forgotten-big-anniversary/story-17892962-detail/story.html17892962 Accessed online, July 2017.

Holt, R. 'The urban transformation in England, 900-1100' in *Anglo-Norman Studies*, 32, 2009, pp. 57-78.

Hurst, H. et al. 'Excavations at Gloucester: Third Interim Report, Kingsholm 1966-75', *Antiquaries Journal* 55.2 (September 1975), pp. 267-94. Published online, 29 November 2011.

Judd, E. 'Women before the Conquest: a Study of Women in Anglo-Saxon England' in *Papers in Women's Studies*, University of Michigan, 1.1, 1974, pp. 127-49.

Karkov, C. 'Aethelflaed's Exceptional Coinage?' in *Old English Newsletter* 29.1, 1995, p.41.

'Millenary of Tamworth Castle: The Celebration. Wonderful Success' in *The Herald*, 12 July 1913, pp. 5,8.

Nielsen, L. 'How dads affect their daughters into adulthood' in *Institute for Family Studies*, June 3 2014. http://family-studies.org/how-dads-affect-their-daughters-into-adulthood/(Accessed on 21 November, 2016).

Shoesmith, R. 'Hereford Saxon defences', *Current Archaeology* 3, 1971, pp. 256-8.

Stafford, P. 'The King's Wife in Wessex, 800–1066' in *New Readings on Women in Old English Literature,* eds. Damico and Hennessy-Olsen, Bloomington, 1990, pp. 56-78.

Thacker, A.T. 'Chester and Gloucester: Early Ecclesiastical Organisation in Two Mercian Burghs' in *Northern History* 18, 1982, pp. 199-211.

'Tigress; Warrior Queen returns to Tamworth Castle', 16 April 2015. http://www.bbc.co.uk/programmes/articles/1QgD6KT7lCJT7K2vWW7jBn9/tigress-warrior-queen-returns-to-tamworth-castle (April 16, 2015. Accessed on 20 November, 2016).

Wainwright, F.T. 'Aethelflaed Lady of the Mercians' in *The Anglo-Saxons: Studies in Some Aspects of their History and Culture, presented to Bruce Dickins*. Clemoes, P., (ed.), London, 1959. Reprinted in *New Readings on Women in Old English Literature,* eds Damico and Hennessy-Olsen, Bloomington, 1990.

Watson, E. 'St Bertelin's Chapel' in *Clas Merdin* http://clasmerdin.blogspot.co.uk/2013

Weiss-McGolerick, E. 'The importance of the father-daughter relationship' in *Parenting*, 11 October 2012. (Accessed November 2016.)

Yorke, B. '"Sisters Under the Skin?": Anglo-Saxon nuns and nunneries in southern England' in *Medieval Women in Southern England, Reading Medieval Studies* 15 (1989), pp. 95-117.

Index

INDEX